ANTHROPOSOPHY
AND THE INNER LIFE
An Esoteric Introduction

by

RUDOLF STEINER

*Nine lectures given to members of the Anthroposophical Society
at the Goetheanum, Dornach, Switzerland,
19th January to 10th February 1924*

RUDOLF STEINER PRESS
ANTHROPOSOPHIC PRESS

Original English language title – *Anthroposophy: An Introduction*

First published 1931
Revised Second Edition 1961
Reprinted 1983
Reprinted 1992 as *Anthroposophy and the Inner Life*
Reprinted 1994

This translation has been made by V. Compton Burnett from the German text (first published in 1927, third edition 1959) entitled *Anthroposophie: eine Einführung in die anthroposophische Weltanschauung.*
Second English edition edited by Owen Barfield and published in agreement with the *Rudolf Steiner Nachlassverwaltung, Dornach, Switzerland.*

Published by Rudolf Steiner Press, P.O. Box 955, Bristol BS99 5QN

All Rights Reserved

© 1994 Rudolf Steiner Press, Bristol

ISBN 85440 387 6

Printed and bound in Great Britain by
The Longdunn Press, Bristol

CONTENTS

ABOUT THE TRANSCRIPTS OF LECTURES

"The results of my anthroposophical work are, first, the books available to the general public; secondly, a great number of lecture-courses, originally regarded as private publications and sold only to members of the Theosophical (later Anthroposophical) Society. The courses consist of more or less accurate notes taken at my lectures, which for lack of time I have not been able to correct. I would have preferred the spoken word to remain the spoken word. But the members wished to have the courses printed for private circulation. Thus they came into existence. Had I been able to correct them the restriction: *for members only* would have been unnecessary from the beginning. As it is, the restriction was dropped more than a year ago.

In my autobiography it is especially necessary to say a word about how my books for the general public on the one hand, and the privately printed courses on the other, belong within what I elaborated as Anthroposophy.

Someone who wishes to trace my inner struggle and effort to present Anthroposophy in a way that is suitable for present-day consciousness must do so through the writings published for general distribution. In these I define my position in relation to the philosophical striving of the present. They contain what to my *spiritual sight* became ever more clearly defined, the edifice of Anthroposophy—certainly incomplete in many ways.

But another requirement arose, different from that of elaborating Anthroposophy and devoting myself solely to problems connected with imparting facts directly from the spiritual world to the general cultural life of today: the requirement of meeting fully the inner need and spiritual longing of the members.

Especially strong were the requests to have light thrown by Anthroposophy upon the Gospels and the Bible in general. The members wished to have courses of lectures on these revelations bestowed upon mankind.

In meeting this need through private lecture courses, another factor arose: at these lectures only members were present. They were familiar with basic content of Anthroposophy. I could address them as people advanced in anthroposophical knowledge. The approach I adopted in these lectures was not at all suitable for the written works intended primarily for the general public.

In these private circles I could formulate what I had to say in a way I should have been *obliged* to modify had it been planned initially for the general public.

Thus the public and the private publications are in fact two quite different things, built upon different foundations. The public writings are the direct result of my inner struggles and labours, whereas the privately printed material includes the inner struggle and labour of the members. I listened to the inner needs of the members, and my living experience of this determined the form of the lectures.

However, nothing was ever said that was not solely the result of my direct experience of the growing content of Anthroposophy. There was never any question of concessions to the prejudices or the preferences of the members. Whoever reads these privately-printed lectures can take them to represent Anthroposophy in the fullest sense. Thus it was possible without hesitation—when the complaints in this direction became too persistent—to depart from the custom of circulating this material only among members. But it must be borne in mind that faulty passages occur in these lecture-reports not revised by myself.

The right to judge such private material can of course, be conceded only to someone who has the pre-requisite basis for such judgment. And in respect of most of this material it would mean *at least* knowledge of man and of the cosmos insofar as these have been presented in the light of Anthroposophy, and also knowledge of what exists as 'anthroposophical history' in what has been imparted from the spiritual world."

Extract from *Rudolf Steiner, An Autobiography*, Chapter 35 pp. 386–388, 2nd Edition 1980, Steinerbooks, New York.

EDITOR'S PREFACE

THIS book is the transcript of a shorthand report of nine lectures given by Rudolf Steiner in the early part of 1924, about a year before he died. Although his audience consisted very largely of people who had been studying for many years the spiritual science which is Steiner's legacy to the world (and which he also called *Anthroposophie*), he himself described the course as an 'Introduction'. The German title of the book is *Anthroposophie: eine Einführung in die Anthroposophische Weltanschauung*. "We will begin again," he observed in Lecture IV, "where we began twenty years ago;" and he may well have had in mind that the Movement itself had, in some sense, begun again only a month or two before with the solemn Foundation of the General Anthroposophical Society under himself as President at Christmas 1923. Though he proceeded *ab initio*, assuming no previous knowledge on the part of his hearers, this course is not an elementary exposition of Anthroposophy. We are gradually led deeply in, and the path is steep towards the end.

There are many very different approaches to the general corpus of revelations or teachings which constitutes Spiritual Science. As with Nature herself, it is often only as the student penetrates deeper and nearer to the centre that any connection between these different approaches become apparent. A reader of *Christianity as Mystical Fact*, for example, which dates from 1902 and of Steiner's lectures on the Gospels might well be surprised to find that it is possible to read *Theosophy* (1904) without ever discovering that the incarnation of Christ and the death on Golgotha are, according to him, the very core of the evolution of

7

the universe and man. The truth is that the mastery of Anthro-posophy involves, for our too stereotyped thinking, something like the learning of a new language. It would be possible to learn to read Greek and only afterwards to discover that the New Testament was written in that tongue.

From this point of view the present book is in the same category as *Theosophy*, yet even within this category the two approaches are made from such diverse directions that one might almost suppose the books to be the work of different men. Nevertheless it is best to look on the following lectures—as Steiner himself makes it clear that he does—as a supplement or complement to what is to be found in *Theosophy*.

The book *Theosophy* is the most systematic of all the writings that Steiner has bequeathed to us. Its whole basis is classification and definition and, taken by itself, it undoubtedly gives (quite apart from the dubious associations which the *word* 'theosophy' has for English ears) a false impression of the nature of Anthro-posophy. It is as indispensable to the student as a good grammar is indispensable to a man engaged in mastering a new language, and it contains as much—and as little—as a grammar does of all that the language can do and say. Its method is that of description from outside. And this approach, essential as it is as one among others, is perhaps the one most likely to lead to misunderstanding and misrepresentation. Such terms as 'soul world', 'spiritland', 'elemental beings', 'aura', are liable to be taken literally in spite of the author's express warnings to the contrary. The descriptions are taken as *reproductions* of the reality that underlies them instead of as similes—attempts, that is, at making clear a purely spiritual reality in words which have received their stamp of significance from their relation to the physical world.

No one who studies the teachings of Rudolf Steiner seriously remains in any real danger of succumbing to this sort of literalness. But anyone reading hurriedly through the book *Theosophy*—or even through *Theosophy* and the *Outline of Occult Science*—and inclined to judge the value of Anthroposophy from that single adventure may well do so. That is why the present book seems to me to be an important one—not only for 'advanced' students of Anthroposophy, to whom it is perhaps primarily addressed, but

8

also to the comparative beginner. It is condensed and difficult for most readers, and above all for those who have never dipped into the broad unbroken stream of books and lectures which flowed from Rudolf Steiner during the twenty years that elapsed between the publication of *Theosophy* and the delivery of this Course. But even if the content is far from fully understood, it cannot fail to give the reader some idea, let us say, of *the sort of thing* that is really signified by the spatial and other physical metaphors in which the systematic exposition of *Theosophy* is couched.

For here the approach is from within. It is no longer simply the objective facts and events, but the way in which the soul tentatively begins to experience these, which the lecturer makes such earnest efforts to convey. We have exchanged a guide book for a book of travel. The one who has been there re-creates his experience for the benefit of those who have not, trying with every device at his disposal to reveal what it actually *felt* like. Of course the difficulty is still there; it can still only be done by metaphor and suggestion; but the difficulty is much less likely to be burked by the reader's surreptitiously substituting in his own imagination a physical or sense-experience for a purely super-sensible one.

Compare, for instance the description of the astral body given in *Theosophy* with the characterisation of it in No. V of these lectures:

One says to oneself: What I am observing as the astral body of this person is not really present today, i.e. on the 2nd February 1924. If the person is twenty years of age, you must go backwards in time—let us say, to January 1904. You perceive that this astral body is really back there, and extends still further back into the unlimited. It has remained there and has not accompanied him through life. Here we have only a kind of appearance—a beam. It is like looking down an avenue; there, in the distance, are the last trees, very close together. Behind them is a source of light. You can have the radiance of the light *here*, but the source is behind—it need not move forward that its light may shine here.

So, too, the astral body has remained behind, and only throws its beam into life. It has really remained in the spiritual world and has not come with us into the physical. In respect

9

to our astral body we always remain before conception and birth, in the spiritual world. If we are twenty years old in 1924, it is as if we were still living spiritually before the year 1904 and, in respect to our astral body, had only stretched forth a feeler.

"Thus," he adds a few pages later, "if you describe the astral body as I have done in my *Theosophy* you must realise, *in order to complete your insight* (my italics)":

> that what is active here is the 'radiance' of something far back in time. The human being is really like a comet stretching its tail far back into the past. It is not possible to obtain a true insight into man's being unless we acquire these new concepts. People who believe one can enter the spiritual world with the same concepts one has for the physical world should become spiritualists, not anthroposophists.

In the same way one could compare the description of the etheric body in the earlier book with its treatment here in Lecture IV. The etheric body is not a vehicle of any such 'life-force', as is understood by the creative evolutionists. It is totally incompatible with the assumptions of positivist science. If it can be described as a 'formative forces' body, it can equally well be described, from another approach, as a thought-body. This is the approach which is required for all the teachings which Steiner developed later concerning the descent of the Cosmic Intelligence and its progressive embodiment in the personal intelligence of man. And it is this approach which is chosen in the book which follows.

He begins by describing the practical steps needed to develop the 'strengthened thinking' which is the first stage of higher knowledge. And he continues:

> If you strengthen your thinking the supra-terrestrial spatial world begins to concern you and the 'second man' you have discovered—just as the earthly, physical world concerned you before. And, as you ascribe the origin of your physical body to the physical earth, you now ascribe your second existence to the cosmic ether through whose activity earthly things become visible. From your own experience you can now speak of

having a physical body *and an etheric body* . . . I stretch out my physical arm and my physical hand takes hold of an object. I feel in a sense the flowing forces in this action. Through strengthening my thought I come to feel that it is inwardly mobile and now induces a kind of 'touching' within me—a 'touching' that also takes place in an organism; this is the etheric organism; that finer, supersensible organism which exists no less than the physical organism, though it is connected with the supra-terrestrial, not the terrestrial.

Equally important is the exposition in this lecture of the way in which astral and etheric find outward expression in the *physical* constitution of man, the etheric in his fluid organisation, which can only be understood with the help of the concept of the etheric body, and the astral in that 'third man'—who is physically the 'airy man' and who can be experienced as 'an inner musical element in the breathing'. The nervous system is shown to be the representation of this inner music.

The matter in this book is extremely condensed and one feels one is maiming it by arbitrary selections such as I am making for the purpose of this Introduction. I have, for instance, said nothing of the extensive and detailed discourse on dreams contained in Lectures VII and VIII, which some readers may even find the most enlightening thing in the book. One final selection may however perhaps be made. In these lectures Steiner approaches the life after death by speaking of 'four phases of memory'. The theme is first heard in Lecture VI, where, after speaking of the nature of memory he emphasises that it is not the concern of the remembering individual alone, but is there for the sake of the universe—"in order that its content may pass through us and be received again in the forms into which we can transmute it".

> The universe needs us because, through us, it 'fulfils' itself —fills itself again and again with its own content. . . . The universe gives its cosmic thoughts to our etheric body and receives them back again in a humanised condition.

It receives them back when we die. The moment we die, the world takes back what it has given. "But it is something new that it receives, for we have experienced it all in a particular way." Then, in the ninth and last lecture, the last three phases of memory lead into—indeed become—in a miracle of condensation—all that is presented so differently in *Theosophy* under such titles as 'The Soul in the Soul-World after Death'.

Is this an esoteric or an exoteric work? Certainly it will be more readily appreciated by readers who have worked through other approaches to be found in the books and lecture-cycles and perhaps especially in the *Leading Thoughts*. Yet it is the whole aim and character of Spiritual Science, as Rudolf Steiner developed it, to endeavour to be esoteric in an exoteric way. For that was what he believed the crisis of the twentieth century demands. And I doubt if he ever struggled harder to combine the two qualities than in these nine lectures given at the end of his life. Thus, although he was addressing members of the Anthroposophical Society, I believe that he had his gaze fixed on Western man in general, and I hope that an increasing number of those who are as yet unacquainted with any of his teaching may find in this book (and it can only be done by intensive application) a convincing proof of the immense fund of wisdom, insight and knowledge from which these teachings spring.

OWEN BARFIELD

London,
August 1960.

Lecture 1

ANTHROPOSOPHY AS WHAT MEN LONG FOR TODAY

19th January, 1924

IN attempting to give a kind of introduction to Anthroposophy I shall try to indicate, as far as possible, the way it can be presented to the world today. Let me begin, however, with some preliminary remarks. We have usually not sufficient regard for the Spiritual as a living reality; and a living reality must be grasped in the fulness of life. Feeling ourselves members of the Anthroposophical Society and the bearers of the Movement, we ought not to act each day on the assumption that the Anthroposophical Movement has just begun. It has, in fact, existed for more than two decades, and the world has taken an attitude towards it. Therefore, in whatever way you come before the world as Anthroposophists, you must bear this in mind. The feeling that the world has already taken up an attitude towards Anthroposophy must be there in the background. If you have not this feeling and think you can simply present the subject in an absolute sense—as one might have done twenty years ago—you will find yourselves more and more presenting Anthroposophy in a false light. This has been done often enough, and it is time it stopped. Our Christmas meeting should mark a beginning in the opposite direction; it must not remain ineffective, as I have already indicated in many different directions.

Of course, we cannot expect every member of the Society to develop, in some way or other, fresh initiative, if he is not so constituted. I might put it this way: Everyone has the right to continue to be a passively interested member, content to receive what is given. But whoever would share, in any way, in putting Anthroposophy before the world, cannot ignore what I have just explained. From now on complete truth must rule in word and deed.

No doubt I shall often repeat such preliminary remarks. We shall now begin a kind of introduction to the anthroposophical view of the world.

Whoever decides to speak about Anthroposophy must assume, to begin with, that what he wants to say is really just what the heart of his listener is itself saying. Indeed, no science based on initiation has ever intended to utter anything except that which was really being spoken by the hearts of those who wished to hear. To meet the deepest needs of the hearts of those requiring Anthroposophy must be, in the fullest sense, the fundamental note of every presentation of it.

.   .   .   .   .

If we observe today those who get beyond the superficial aspect of life, we find that ancient feelings, present in every human soul from age to age, have revived. In their subconscious life the men and women of today harbour earnest questions. They cannot even express these in clear thoughts, much less find answers in what the civilised world can offer; but these questions are there, and a large number of people feel them deeply. In fact, these questions are present today in all who really think. But when we formulate them in words they appear, at first, far-fetched. Yet they are so near, so intimately near to the soul of every thinking man.

We can start with *two questions* chosen from all the riddles oppressing man today. The first presents itself to man's soul when he contemplates the world around him and his own human existence. He sees human beings enter earthly life through birth; he sees life running its course between birth (or conception) and physical death, and subject to the most manifold experiences, inner and outer; and he sees external nature with all the fullness of impressions that confront man and gradually fill his soul.

There is the human soul in a human body. It sees one thing before all others: that Nature receives into herself all the human soul perceives of physical, earthly existence. When man has passed through the gate of death, Nature receives the human body through one element or another (it makes little difference whether

14

through burial or cremation). And what does Nature do with this physical body? She destroys it. We do not usually study the paths taken by the individual substances of the body. But if we make observations at places where a peculiar kind of burial has been practised, we deepen this impression made by a study of what Nature does with the physical, sensible part of man, when he has passed through the gate of death. You know there are subterranean vaults where human remains are kept isolated, but not from the air. They dry up. And what remains after a certain time? A distorted human form consisting of carbonate of lime, itself inwardly disintegrated. This mass of carbonate of lime still resembles, in a distorted form, the human body, but if you only shake it a little, it falls to dust.

This helps us to realise vividly the experience of the soul on seeing what happens to the physical instrument with which man does all things between birth and death. We then turn to Nature, to whom we owe all our knowledge and insight, and say: Nature, who produces from her womb the most wonderful crystal forms, who conjures forth each spring the sprouting, budding plants, who maintains for decades the trees with their bark, and covers the earth with animal species of the most diverse kinds, from the largest beasts to the tiniest bacilli, who lifts her waters to the clouds and upon whom the stars send down their mysterious rays—how is this realm of Nature related to what man, as part of her, carries with him between birth and death? She destroys it, reduces it to formless dust. For man, Nature with her laws is the destroyer. Here, on the one hand, is the human form; we study it in all its wonder. It is, indeed, wonderful, for it is more perfect than any other form to be found on earth. There, on the other hand, is Nature with her stones, plants, animals, clouds, rivers and mountains, with all that rays down from the sea of stars, with all that streams down, as light and warmth, from the sun to the earth. Yet this Realm of Nature cannot suffer the human form within her own system of laws.* The human

---

* This sentence and the rest of the paragraph in which it occurs must of course be read in the context of the lecture as a whole. Taken by itself it may well arouse the objection: "The human form is as much within Nature's system of laws as those of the plants and animals. Certainly Nature destroys

being before us is reduced to dust when given to her charge. We see all this. We do not form ideas about it, but it is deeply rooted in our feeling life. Whenever we stand in the presence of death, this feeling takes firm root in mind and heart. It is not from a merely selfish feeling nor from a merely superficial hope of survival, that a subconscious question takes shape in mind and heart—a question of infinite significance for the soul, determining its happiness and unhappiness, even when not expressed in words. All that makes, for our conscious life, the happiness or unhappiness of our earthly destiny, is trivial in comparison with the uncertainty of feeling engendered by the sight of death. For then the question takes shape: Whence comes this human form? I look at the wonderfully formed crystal, at the forms of plants and animals. I see the rivers winding their way over the earth, I see the mountains, and all that the clouds reveal and the stars send down to earth. I see all this—man says to himself—but the human form can come from none of these. These have only destructive forces for the human form, forces that turn it to dust.

In this way the anxious question presents itself to the human mind and heart: Where, then, is the world from which the human form comes? And at the sight of death, too, the anxious question arises: Where is the world, that other world, from which the human form comes?

Do not say, my dear friends, that you have not yet heard this question formulated in this way. If you only listen to what people put into words out of the consciousness of their heads, you will not hear it. But if you approach people and they put before you the complaints of their hearts, you can, if you understand the heart's language, hear it asking from its unconscious life: Where is the other world from which the human form comes?—for man, with his form, does not belong to this. People often reveal the complaints of their hearts by seizing on some triviality of life,

it after death; but does she not also bring it to birth?" It may help to remind the reader that Dr. Steiner is at this stage merely putting into words a *feeling*, which, he expressly says, arises *when we stand in the presence of death*. Later on in the book, when he deals with the relation in which the human body stands to the world of nature, he shows how the human form in fact has an origin quite different from those of other living creatures.—*Editor*.

considering it from various points of view and allowing such considerations to colour the whole question of their destiny.

Thus man is confronted by the world he sees, senses and studies, and about which he constructs his science. It provides him with the basis for his artistic activities and the grounds for his religious worship. It confronts him; and he stands on the earth, feeling in the depths of his soul: I do not belong to this world; there must be another from whose magic womb I have sprung in my present form. To what world do I belong? This sounds in men's hearts today. It is a comprehensive question; and if men are not satisfied with what the sciences give them, it is because this question is there and the sciences are far from touching it. Where is the world to which man really belongs?—for it is not the visible world.

My dear friends, I know quite well it is not I who have spoken these words. I have only formulated what human hearts are saying. That is the point. It is not a matter of bringing men something unknown to their own souls. A person who does this may work sensationally; but for us it can only be a matter of putting into words what human souls themselves are saying. What we perceive of our own bodies, or of another's, in so far as it is visible, has no proper place in the rest of the visible world. We might say: No finger of my body really belongs to the visible world, for this contains only destructive forces for every finger.

So, to begin with, man stands before the great Unknown, but must regard himself as a part of it. In respect of all that is *not* man, there is—spiritually—light around him; the moment he looks back upon himself, the whole world grows dark, and he gropes in the darkness, bearing with him the riddle of his own being. And it is the same when man regards himself from outside, finding himself an external being within Nature; he cannot, as a human being, contact this world.

Further: not our heads but the depths of our subconscious life put questions subsidiary to the general question I have just discussed. In contemplating his life in the physical world, which is his instrument between birth and death, man realises he could not live at all without borrowing continually from this visible world. Every bit of food I put into my mouth, every sip of water comes from the visible world to which I do not belong at all. I cannot live without this world; and yet, if I have just eaten a morsel of some substance (which must, of course, be a part of the visible world) and pass immediately afterwards through the gate of death, this morsel becomes at once part of the destructive forces of the visible world. It does not do so within me while I live; hence my own being must be preserving it therefrom. Yet my own being is nowhere to be found outside, in the visible world. What, then, do I do with the morsel of food, the drink of water, I take into my mouth? Who am I who receive the substances of Nature and transform them? Who am I? This is the second question and it arises from the first.

When I enter into relationship with the visible world I not only walk in darkness, I act in the dark without knowing who is acting, or who the being is that I designate as myself. I surrender to the visible world, yet I do not belong to it.

All this lifts man out of the visible world, letting him appear to himself as a member of a quite different one. But the great riddle, the anxious doubt confronts him: Where is the world to which I belong? The more human civilisation has advanced and men have learnt to think intensively, the more anxiously have they felt this question. It is deep-seated in men's hearts today, and divides the civilised world into two classes. There are those who repress this question, smother it, do not bring it to clarity within them. But they suffer from it nevertheless, as from a terrible longing to solve this riddle of man. Others deaden themselves in face of this question, doping themselves with all sorts of things in outer life. But in so deadening themselves they kill within them the secure feeling of their own being. Emptiness comes over their souls. This feeling of emptiness is present in the subconsciousness of countless human beings today.

This is one side—the one great question with the subsidiary question mentioned. It presents itself when man looks at himself from outside, and only dimly, subconsciously, perceives his relation, as a human being between birth and death, to the world.

The other question presents itself when man looks into his own inner being. Here is the other pole of human life. Thoughts are here, copying external Nature which man represents to himself through them. He develops sensations and feelings about the outer world and acts upon it through his will. In the first place, he looks back upon this inner being of his, and the surging waves of thinking, feeling and willing confront him. So he stands with his soul in the present. But, in addition, there are the memories of experiences undergone, memories of what he has seen earlier in his present life. All these fill his soul. But what are they? Well, man does not usually form clear ideas of what he thus retains within him, but his subconsciousness does form such ideas.

Now a single attack of migraine that dispels his thoughts, makes his inner being at once a riddle. His condition every time he sleeps, lying motionless and unable to relate himself, through his senses, to the outer world, makes his inner being a riddle again. Man feels his physical body must be active and then thoughts, feelings and impulses of will arise in his soul. I turn from the stone I have just been observing and which has, perhaps, this or that crystalline form; after a little time I turn to it again. It remains as it was. My thought, however, arises, appears as an image in my soul, and fades away. I feel it to be infinitely more valuable than the muscles or bones I bear in my body. Yet it is a mere fleeting image; nay, it is less than the picture on my wall, for this will persist for a time until its substance crumbles away My thought, however, flits past—a picture that continually comes and goes, content to be merely a picture. And when I look into the inner being of my soul, I find nothing but these pictures (or mental presentations). I must admit that my soul life consists of them.

I look at the stone again. It is out there in space; it persists. I picture it to myself now, in an hour's time, in two hours' time. In the meantime the thought disappears and must always be renewed. The stone, however, remains outside. What sustains the stone from hour to hour? What lets the thought of it fluctuate from hour to hour? What maintains the stone from hour to hour? What annihilates the thought again and again so that it must be kindled anew by outer perception? We say the stone 'exists'; existence is to be ascribed to it. Existence, however, cannot be ascribed to the thought. Thought can grasp the colour and the form of the stone, but not that whereby the stone exists as a stone. That remains external to us, only the mere picture entering the soul.

It is the same with every single thing of external Nature in relation to the human soul. In his soul, which man can regard as his own inner being, the whole of Nature is reflected. Yet he has only fleeting pictures—skimmed off, as it were, from the surfaces of things; into these pictures the inner being of things does not enter. With my mental pictures (or presentations) I pass through the world, skimming everywhere the surfaces of things. What the things are, however, remains outside. The external world does not contact what is within me.

Now, when man, in the sight of death, confronts the world around him in this way he must say: My being does not belong to this world, for I cannot contact it as long as I live in a physical body. Moreover, when my body contacts this outer world after death, every step it takes means destruction. There, outside, is the world. If man enters it fully, he is destroyed; it does not suffer his inner being within it. Nor can the outer world enter man's soul. Thoughts are images and remain outside the real existence of things. The being of stones, the being of plants, of animals, stars and clouds—these do not enter the human soul Man is surrounded by a world which cannot enter his soul but remains outside.

On the one hand, man remains outside Nature. This becomes clear to him at the sight of death. On the other hand, Nature remains external to his soul.

Regarding himself as an object, man is confronted by the anxious question about another world. Contemplating what is most intimate in his own inner being—his thoughts, mental images, sensations, feelings and impulses of will—he sees that Nature, in whom he lives, remains external to them all. He does not possess her.

Here is the sharp boundary between man and Nature. Man cannot approach Nature without being destroyed; Nature cannot enter the inner being of man without becoming a mere semblance. When man projects himself in thought into Nature, he is compelled to picture his own destruction; and when he looks into himself, asking: How is Nature related to my soul? he finds only the empty semblance of Nature.

Nevertheless, while man bears within him this semblance of

the minerals, plants, animals, stars, suns, clouds, mountains and rivers, while he bears within his memory the semblance of the experiences he has undergone with these kingdoms of Nature, experiencing all this in his fluctuating inner world, his own sense of being emerges amid it all.

How is this? How does man experience this sense of his own existence? He experiences it somewhat as follows. Perhaps it can only be expressed in a picture:

Imagine we are looking at a wide ocean. The waves rise and fall. There is a wave here, a wave there; there are waves everywhere, due to the heaving water. One particular wave, however, holds our attention, for we see that something is living in it, that it is not merely surging water. Yet water surrounds this living something on all sides. We only know that something is living in this wave, though even here we can only see the enveloping water. This wave looks like the others; but the strength of its surging, the force with which it rises, gives an impression of something special living within. This wave disappears and reappears at another place; again the water conceals what is animating it from within. So it is with the soul life of man. Images, thoughts, feelings and impulses of will surge up; waves everywhere. One of the waves emerges in a thought, in a feeling, in an act of volition. The ego is within, but concealed by the thoughts, or feelings, or impulses of will, as the water conceals what is living in the wave. At the place where man can only say: "There my own self surges up," he is confronted by mere semblance; he does not know what he himself is. His true being is certainly there and is inwardly felt and experienced, but this 'semblance' in the soul conceals it, as the water of the wave the unknown living thing from the depths of the sea. Man feels his own true being hidden by the unreal images of his own soul. Moreover, it is as if he wanted continually to hold fast to his own existence, as if he would lay hold of it at some point, for he knows it is there. Yet, at the very moment when he would grasp it, it eludes him. Man is not able, within the fluctuating life of his soul, to grasp the real being he knows himself to be. And when he discovers that this surging, unreal life of his soul has something to do with that other world presented by nature, he is more than ever perplexed. The riddle of nature is, at least, one that is present in experience; the riddle of man's own soul is not present in experience because it is itself alive. It is, so to speak, a living riddle, for it answers man's constant question: "What am I?" by putting a mere semblance before him.

On looking into his own inner being man receives the continual answer: I only show you a semblance of yourself; and if you ascribe a spiritual origin to yourself, I only show you a semblance of this spiritual existence within your soul life.

Thus, from two directions, searching questions confront man today. One of these questions arises when he becomes aware that:

Nature exists, but man can only approach her by letting her destroy him;

the other when he sees:

The human soul exists, but Nature can only approach this human soul by becoming mere semblance.

These two truths live in the subconsciousness of man today. On the one hand, we have the unknown world of Nature, the destroyer of man; on the other, the unreal image of the human soul which Nature cannot approach although man can only complete his physical existence by co-operating with her. Man stands, so to speak, in double darkness, and the question arises:

Where is the other world to which I belong?

Man turns, now, to historical tradition, to what has been handed down from ancient times and lives on. He learns that there was once a science that spoke of this unknown world. He looks to ancient times and feels deep reverence for what they tried to teach about the other world within the world of Nature. If one only knows how to deal with Nature in the right way, this other world is revealed to human gaze.

But modern consciousness has discarded this ancient knowledge. It is no longer regarded as valid. It has been handed down to us, but is no longer believed. Man can no longer feel sure that the knowledge acquired by the men of an ancient epoch as their science can answer today his own anxious question arising from the above subconscious facts.

22

So we turn to Art.

But here again we find something significant. The artistic treatment of physical material—spiritualisation of physical matter—comes down to us from ancient times. Much of this treatment has been retained and can be learnt from tradition. Nevertheless, it is just the man with a really artistic subconscious nature who feels most dissatisfied today; for he can no longer realise what Raphael could still conjure into the human earthly form—the reflection of another world to which man truly belongs. Where is the artist today who can handle earthly, physical substance in such an artistic way?

Thirdly, there is Religion. This, too, has been handed down through tradition from olden times. It directs man's feeling and devotion to that other world. It arose in a past age through man receiving the revelations of the realm of Nature which is really so foreign to him. For, if we turn our spiritual gaze backwards over thousands of years, we find human beings who also felt: Nature exists, but man can only approach her by letting her destroy him.

Indeed, the men who lived thousands of years ago felt this in the depths of their souls. They looked at the corpse passing over into external Nature as into a vast Moloch, and saw it destroyed. But they also saw the human soul passing through the same portal beyond which the body is destroyed. Even the Egyptians saw this, or they would never have embalmed their dead. They saw the soul go further still. These men of ancient times felt that the soul grows greater and greater, and passes into the cosmos. And then they saw the soul, which had disappeared into the elements, return again from the cosmic spaces, from the stars. They saw the human soul vanish at death—at first through the gate of death, then on the way to the other world, then returning from the stars. Such was the ancient religion: a cosmic revelation—cosmic revelation from the hour of death, cosmic revelation from the hour of birth. The words have been retained; the belief has been retained, but has its content still any relation to the cosmos? It is preserved in religious literature, in religious tradition foreign to the world.

The man of our present civilisation can no longer see any

23

relation between what religious tradition has handed down to him and the anxious question confronting him today. He looks at Nature and only sees the human physical body passing through the gate of death and falling a prey to destruction. He sees, moreover, the human form enter through the gate of birth, and is compelled to ask whence it comes. Wherever he looks, he cannot find the answer. He no longer sees it coming from the stars, as he is no longer able to see it after death. So religion has become an empty word.

Thus, in his civilisation, man has around him what ancient times possessed as science, art and religion. But the science of the ancients has been discarded, their art is no longer felt in its inwardness, and what takes its place today is something man is not able to lift above physical matter, making this a vehicle for the radiant expression of the spiritual.

The religious element has remained from olden times. It has, however, no point of contact with the world, for, in spite of it the above riddle of the relation of the world to man remains. Man looks into his inner being, and hears the voice of conscience; but in olden times this was the voice of that God who guided the soul through those regions in which the body is destroyed, and led it again to earthly life, giving it its appropriate form. It was this God who spoke in the soul as the voice of conscience. Today even the voice of conscience has become external, and moral laws are no longer traceable to divine impulses. Man surveys history, to begin with; he studies what has come down from olden times, and—at most—can dimly feel: The ancients experienced the two great riddles of existence differently from the way I feel them today. For this reason they could answer them in a certain way. I can no longer answer them. They hover before me and oppress my soul, for they only show me my destruction after death and the semblance of reality during life.

It is thus that man confronts the world today. From this mood of soul arise the questions Anthroposophy has to answer. Human hearts are speaking in the way we have described and asking where they can find that knowledge of the world which meets their needs.

Anthroposophy comes forward as such knowledge, and would

speak about the world and man so that such knowledge may arise again—knowledge that can be understood by modern consciousness, as ancient science, art and religion were understood by ancient consciousness. Anthroposophy receives íts mighty task from the voice of the human heart itself, and is no more than what humanity is longing for today. Because of this, Anthroposophy will have to live. It answers to what man most fervidly longs for, both for his outer and inner life. "Can there be such a world-conception today?" one may ask. The Anthroposophical Society has to supply the answer. It must find the way to let the hearts of men speak from out of their deepest longings; then they will experience the deepest longing for the answers.

Lecture 2

MEDITATION

20th January, 1924

YESTERDAY I had to show how we can observe ourselves in two ways, and how the riddle of the world and of man confronts us from both directions. If we look once more at what we found yesterday, we see, on the one hand, the human physical body, perceived—at first—in the same way as the external, physical world. We call it the physical body because it stands before our physical senses just as the external, physical world. At the same time, however, we must call to mind the great difference between the two. Indeed, yesterday we had to recognise this great difference from the fact that man, on passing through the gate of death, must surrender his physical body to the elements of the external, physical world; and these destroy it. The action of external Nature upon the human physical body is destructive, not constructive. So we must look quite outside the physical world for what gives the human physical body its shape between birth (or conception) and death. We must speak, to begin with, of another world which builds up this human body that external, physical Nature can only destroy.

On the other hand there are two considerations which show the close relationship between the human physical body and Nature. In the first place, the body requires substances—building materials in a sense—although this is not strictly accurate. Let us say, it has need of the substances of external nature, or, at least, needs to take them in.

Again: when we observe the external manifestations of the physical body—whether it be its excretions, or the whole body as seen after death—it is nevertheless substances of the external, physical world that we observe. We always find the same sub-

26

stances as in the external, physical world—whether we are studying the separate excretions or the whole physical body cast off at death.

So we are compelled to say: Whatever the inner processes going on in the human body may be, their beginning and end are related to the external, physical world.

Materialistic science, however, draws from this fact a conclusion that cannot be drawn at all. Though we see how man, through eating, drinking and breathing, takes in substances from the external physical world and gives these same substances back again, in expiration, in excretion or at death, we can only say that we have here to do with a beginning and an end. We have not determined the intermediary processes within the physical body.

We speak so glibly of the blood man bears within him; but has anyone ever investigated the blood within the living human organism itself? This cannot be done with physical means at all. We have no right to draw the materialistic conclusion that what enters the body and leaves it again was also within it.

In any case, we see an immediate transformation when external, physical substances are taken in—let us say, by the mouth. We need only put a small grain of salt in the mouth and it is at once dissolved. The transformation is immediate. The physical body of man is not the same, in its inner nature, as the external world; it transforms what it takes in, and then transforms it back again. Thus we must seek for something within the human organism that is, at first, similar to external nature and, on excretion, becomes so again. It is what lies between these two stages that we must first discover.

Try to picture this that I have said: On the one hand, we have what the organism takes in; on the other, what it gives off—including even the physical body as a whole. Between these are the processes within the organism itself. From the study of what the human physical organism takes in we can say nothing at all about the relation of man to external nature. We might put it this way: Though external physical nature does destroy man's corpse, dissolving and dissipating it, man does, with his organism, 'get even' with Nature. He dissolves everything he receives from

27

her. Thus, when we commence with man's organs of assimilation, we find no relationship to external nature, for this is destroyed by them. We only find such a relationship when we turn to what man excretes. In relation to the form man bears into physical life, Nature is a destroyer; in regard to what man casts off, Nature receives what the human organism provides. Thus the human physical organism comes eventually to be very unlike itself and to resemble external Nature very much. It does this through excretion.

If you think this over you will say to yourself: There, outside, are the substances of the different kingdoms of Nature. They are, today, just what they have become; but they have certainly not always been as they are. Even physical science admits that past conditions of the earth were very different from those of today. What we see around us in the kingdoms of Nature has only gradually become what it is. And when we look at man's physical body we see it destroys—or transforms—what it takes in. (We shall see that it really destroys, but for the moment we will say 'transforms'.) At any rate, what is taken in must be reduced to a certain condition from which it can be led back again to present physical Nature. In other words: If you think of a beginning somewhere in the human organism, where the substances begin to develop in the direction of excretions, and then think of the earth, you are led to trace it back to a similar condition in which it once was. You have to say: At some past time the whole earth must have been in the condition in which something within man is today; and in the short space of time during which something incorporated into the human organism is transformed into excretory products, the inner processes of the organism recapitulate what the earth itself has accomplished in the course of long ages.

Thus we look at external Nature today and see that it was once something very different. But when we try to find something similar to its former condition we have to look into our own organism. The beginning of the earth is still there. Every time we eat, the substances of our food are transformed into a condition in which the whole earth once was. The earth has developed further in the course of long periods of time and become what it is today; our food substances, in developing to the point of excretion, give a brief recapitulation of the whole earth-process.

Now, you can look at the vernal point of the zodiac, where the sun rises every spring. This point is not stationary; it is advancing. In the Egyptian epoch, for example, it was in the constellation of Taurus. It has advanced through Taurus and Aries, and is today in the constellation of Pisces; and it is still advancing. It moves in a circle and will return after a certain time. Though this point where the sun rises in spring describes a complete circle in the heavens in 25,920 years, the sun describes this circle every day. It rises and sets, thereby describing the same path as the vernal point. Let us contemplate, on the one hand, the long epoch of 25,920 years, which is the time taken by the vernal point to complete its path; and on the other hand, the short period of twenty-four hours in which the sun rises, sets and rises again at the same point. The sun describes the same circle. It is similar with the human physical organism. Through long periods the earth consisted of substances like those within us at a certain stage of digestion—the stage midway between ingestion and egestion, when the former passes over into the latter. Here we carry within us the beginning of the earth. In a short period of time we reach the excretory stage, in which we resemble the earth; we hand over substances to the earth in the form they have today. In our digestive processes we do in the physical body something similar to what the sun does in its diurnal round with respect to the vernal point. Thus we may survey the physical globe and say: Today this physical globe has reached a condition in which its laws destroy the form of our physical organism. But this earth must once have been in a condition in which it was subjected to other laws—laws which, today, bring our physical organism into the condition of food-stuffs midway between ingestion and egestion. That is to say, we bear within us the laws of the earth's beginning; we recapitulate what was once on the earth.

You see, we may regard our physical organism as organised for taking in external substances—present-day substances—and excreting them again as such; but it bears within it something that was present in the beginning of the earth but which the earth no longer has. This has disappeared from the earth leaving only the final products, not the initial substances. Thus we bear within us something to be sought for in very ancient times within the constitution of the earth. It is what we thus bear within us, and the earth as a whole has not got, that raises us above physical, earthly life. It leads man to say: I have preserved within me the beginning of the earth. Through entering physical existence through birth, I have ever within me something the earth had millions of years ago, but has no longer.

From this you see that, in calling man a microcosm, we cannot merely take account of the world around us today. We must go beyond its present condition and consider past stages of its evolution. To understand man we must study primeval conditions of the earth.

What the earth no longer possesses but man still has in this way, can become an object of observation. We must have recourse to what may be called meditation. We are accustomed merely to allow the 'ideas' or, mental presentations [Vorstellungen], whereby we perceive the world, to arise within us—merely to represent the outer world to ourselves with the help of such ideas. And for the last few centuries man has become so accustomed to copy merely the outer world in his ideas, that he does not realise his power of also forming ideas freely from within. To do this is to meditate; it is to fill one's consciousness with ideas not derived from external Nature, but called up from within. In doing so we pay special attention to the inner activity involved. In this way one comes to feel that there is really a 'second man' within, that there is something in man that can really be inwardly felt and experienced—just as, for example, the force of the muscles when we stretch out an arm. We experience this muscular force; but when we think we ordinarily experience nothing. Through meditation, however, it is possible so to strengthen our power of thinking—the power whereby we form thoughts—that we experience this power inwardly, even as we experience the force of our muscles on stretching out an arm. Our meditation is successful when we are at length able to say: In my ordinary thinking I am really quite passive. I allow something to happen to me; I let Nature fill me with thoughts. But I will no longer let myself be filled with thoughts, I will place in my consciousness the thoughts I want to have, and will only pass from one thought to another through the force of inner thinking itself. In this way our thinking becomes stronger and stronger, just as the force of our muscles grows stronger if we use our arms. At length we notice that this thinking activity is a 'tension', a 'touching', an inner experience, like the experience of our own muscular force. When we have so strengthened ourselves within that our thinking has this character, we are at once confronted in our consciousness by what we carry within us as a repetition of an ancient condition of the earth. We learn to know the force that transforms food substances within the body and retransforms them again. And in experiencing this higher man within, who is as real as the physical man himself, we come, at the same time, to perceive with our strengthened thinking the external things of the world.

Suppose, my dear friends, I look at a stone with such strengthened thinking. Let us say it is a crystal of salt or of quartz. It seems to me like meeting a man I have already seen. I am reminded of experiences I had with him ten or twenty years ago. In the meantime he may have been in Australia, or anywhere, but the man before me now conjures up the experience I had with him ten or twenty years ago. So, if I look at a crystal of salt or of quartz with this strengthened thinking, there immediately comes before my mind the past state of the crystal, like the memory of a primeval condition of the earth. At that time the crystal of salt was not hexahedral, i.e. six-faced, for it was all part of a surging, weaving, cosmic sea of rock. The primeval condition of the earth comes before me, as a memory is evoked by present objects.

I now look again at man, and the very same impression that the primeval condition of the earth made upon me, is now made by the 'second human being' man carries within him. Further: the very same impression is made upon me when I behold, not stones, but plants. Thus I am led to speak, with some justification, of an 'etheric body' as well as the physical. Once the earth was ether; out of this ether it has become what it is today in its inorganic, lifeless constituents. The plants, however, still bear within them the former primeval condition of the earth. And I myself bear within me, as a second man, the human 'etheric body'.

All that I am describing to you can become an object of study

31

for strengthened thinking. So we may say that, if a man takes trouble to develop such thinking he perceives, besides the physical, the etheric in himself, in plants and in the memory of primeval ages evoked by minerals.

Now, what do we learn from this higher kind of observation? We learn that the earth was once in an etheric condition, that the ether has remained and still permeates the plants, the animals—for we can perceive it in them too—and the human being.

But now something further is revealed. We see the minerals free from ether, and the plants endowed with it. At the same time, however, we learn to see ether everywhere. It is still there today, filling cosmic space. In the external, mineral kingdom alone it plays no part; still, it is everywhere. When I simply lift this piece of chalk, I observe all sorts of things happening in the ether. Indeed, lifting a piece of chalk is a complicated process. My hand develops a certain force, but this force is only present in me in the waking state, not when I am asleep. If I follow what the ether does in transmuting food-stuffs, I find this going on during both waking and sleeping states. One might doubt this in the case of man, if one were superficial, but not in the case of snakes; they sleep in order to digest. But what takes place through my raising an arm can only take place in the waking state. The etheric body gives no help here. Nevertheless if I only lift the chalk I must overcome etheric forces—I must work upon the ether. My own etheric body cannot do this. I must bear within me a 'third man' who can.

Now this third man who can move, who can lift things, including his own limbs is not to be found—to begin with—in anything similar in external Nature. Nevertheless external Nature, which is everywhere permeated by ether, enters into relation with this 'force-man'—let us call him—into whom man himself pours the force of his will.

At first it is only in inner experience that we can become aware of this inner unfolding of forces. If, however, we pursue meditation further, not only forming our ideas ourselves, and passing from one idea to another in order to strengthen our thinking, but eliminating again the strengthened thinking so acquired—i.e. emptying our consciousness—we attain something special. Of course, if one frees oneself of ordinary thoughts passively acquired, one falls asleep. The moment one ceases to perceive or think, sleep ensues, for ordinary consciousness is passively acquired. If, however, we develop the forces whereby the etheric is perceived, we have a strengthened man within us; we feel our own thinking forces as we usually feel our muscular forces. And now, when we deliberately eliminate, 'suggest away' this strengthened man we do not fall asleep, but expose our empty consciousness to the world. What we dimly feel when we move our arms, or walk, when we unfold our will, enters us objectively. The forces at work here are nowhere to be found in the world of space; but they enter space when we produce empty consciousness in the way described. We then discover, objectively, this third man within us. Looking now at external Nature we observe that men, animals and plants have etheric bodies, while minerals have not. The latter only remind us of the original 'ether' of the earth. Nevertheless there is ether wherever we turn, though it does not always reveal itself as such.

You see, if you confront plants with the 'meditative' consciousness I described at first, you perceive an etheric image; likewise if you confront a human being. But if you confront the universal ether it is as if you were swimming in the sea. There is only ether everywhere. It gives you no 'picture.' But the moment I merely lift this piece of chalk there appears an image in the etheric where my third man is unfolding his forces.

Picture this to yourselves: The chalk is, at first, there. My hand now takes hold of the chalk and lifts it up. (I could represent the whole process in a series of snapshots.) All this, however, has its counterpart in the ether, though this cannot be seen until I am able to perceive by means of 'empty consciousness'—i.e. until I am able to perceive the third man, not the second. That is to say, the universal ether does not *act* as ether, but in the way the third man acts.

Thus I may say: I have first my physical body (oval),* then my

---

* The drawings in this volume are reconstructions of those freely drawn by Rudolf Steiner in coloured chalks on the blackboard. Some were made progressively but as depicted here they are from the completed sketches. Reproduction in colour is impracticable.

etheric body, perceived in 'meditative' consciousness (yellow), then the third man, which I will call the 'astral' man (red). Everywhere around me I have what we found to be the second thing in the universe—the universal ether (yellow). This, to begin with, is like an indefinite sea of ether.

(*rot* - red; *gelb* - yellow)

Now the moment I radiate into this ether anything that proceeds from this third man within me, it responds; this ether responds as if it were like the third man within me, i.e. not etherically, but 'astrally'. Thus I release through my own activity something within this wide sea of ether that is similar to my own 'third man'.

What is this that acts in the ether as a counter-image? I lift the chalk; my hand moves from below upwards. The etheric picture, however, moves from above downwards; it is an exact counter-image. It is really an astral picture, a mere *picture*. Nevertheless, it is through the real, present-day man that this picture is evoked. Now, if I learn, by means of what I have already described, to

34

look backwards in earth-evolution—if I learn to apply to cosmic evolution what is briefly recapitulated in the way described—I discover the following:

(*Astralleib*—Astral body; *Aethererde*—Etheric earth; *Erde*—Earth)

Here is the present condition of the earth. I go back to an etheric earth. I do not find there, as yet, what has been released through me in the surrounding ether. I must go farther back to a still earlier condition of the earth in which the earth resembled my own astral body. The earth was then astral—a being like my third man. I must look for this being in times long past, in times long anterior to those in which the earth was etheric. Going backwards in time is really no different from seeing a distant object—a light, let us say—that shines as far as this. It is over there, but shines as far as here; it sends images to us here. Now put time instead of space: That which is of like nature with my own astral body was there in primeval times. Time has not ceased to be; it is still there. Just as, in space, light can shine as far as here, so that which lies in a long gone past works on into the present. Fundamentally speaking, the whole time-evolution is still there. Whatever was once there—and is of like nature with that which, in the outer ether, resembles my own astral body—has not disappeared.

Here I touch on something that, spiritually, is actively present and makes *time* into *space*. It is really no different from communi-

35

cating over a long distance with the help of a telegraph. In lifting the chalk I evoke a picture in the ether and communicate with what, for outer perception, has long passed away.

We see how man is placed in the world in a quite different way from what appears at first. And we understand, too, why cosmic riddles present themselves to him. He feels within that he has an etheric body, though he does not realise it clearly: even science does not realise it clearly today. He feels that this etheric body transforms his food-stuffs and transforms them back again. He does not find this in stones, though the stones were already there, in primeval times which he discovers, there as general ether. But in this ether a still more remote past is active. Thus man bears within him an ancient past in a twofold way; a more recent past in his etheric body and a more ancient past in his astral body.

When man confronts Nature today he usually only studies what is lifeless. Even what is living in plants is only studied by applying to them the laws of substances as discovered in his laboratory. He omits to study growth; he neglects the life in his plants. Present-day science really studies plants as one who picks up a book and observes the forms of the letters, but does not read. Science, today, studies all things in this way.

Indeed, if you open a book but cannot read, the forms must appear very puzzling. You cannot really understand why there is here a form like this: 'b', then 'a', then 'l', then 'd', i.e. bald. What are these forms doing side by side? That is, indeed, a riddle. The way of regarding things that I have put before you is really learning to read in the world and in man. By 'learning to read' we come gradually near to the solution of our riddles.

You see, my dear friends, I wanted to put before you merely a general path for human thinking along which one can escape from the condition of despair in which man finds himself and which I described at the outset. We shall proceed to study how one can advance farther and farther in reading the phenomena in the outer world and in man.

In doing this, however, we are led along paths of thought with which man is quite unfamiliar today. And what usually happens? People say: I don't understand that. But what does this mean? It only means that this does not agree with what was taught them at school, and they have become accustomed to think in the way they were trained. "But do not our schools take their stand on genuine science?" Yes, but what does that mean? My dear friends, I will give you just one example of this genuine science.—One who is no longer young has experienced many things like this. One learnt, for example, that various substances are necessary for the process referred to today—the taking in of foodstuffs and their transformation within the human organism. Albumens (proteins), fats, water, salts, sugar and starch products were cited as necessary for men. Then experiments were made.

If we go back twenty years, we find that experiments showed man to require at least one hundred and twenty grammes of protein a day; otherwise he could not live. That was 'science' twenty years ago. What is 'science' today? Today twenty to fifty grammes are sufficient. At that time it was 'science' that one would become ill—under-nourished—if one did not get these one hundred and twenty grammes of protein. Today science says it is injurious to one's health to take more than fifty grammes at the most; one can get along quite well with twenty grammes. If one takes more, putrefying substances form in the intestines and auto-intoxication, self-poisoning, is set up. Thus it is harmful to take more than fifty grammes of protein. That is science today.

This, however, is not merely a scientific question, it has a bearing on life. Just think: twenty years ago, when it was scientific to believe that one must have one hundred and twenty grammes of protein, people were told to choose their diet accordingly. One had to assume that a man could pay for all this. So the question touched the economic sphere. It was proved carefully that it is impossible to obtain these one hundred and twenty grammes of protein from plants. Today we know that man gets the requisite amount of protein from any kind of diet. If he simply eats sufficient potatoes—he need not eat many—along with a little butter, he obtains the requisite amount of protein. Today it is scientifically certain that this is so. Moreover, it is a fact that a man who fills himself with one hundred and twenty grammes of protein acquires a very uncertain appetite. If, on the other hand, he keeps to a diet which provides him with twenty grammes of

37

protein, and happens, once in a while, to take food with less, and which would therefore under-nourish him, he turns from it. His instinct in regard to food becomes reliable. Of course, there are still under-nourished people, but this has other causes and certainly does not come from a deficiency of protein. On the other hand, there are certainly numerous people suffering from auto-intoxication and many other things because they are over-fed with protein.

I do not want to speak now of infectious diseases, but will just mention that people are most susceptible to so-called infection when they take one hundred and twenty grammes of protein [a day]. They are then most likely to get diphtheria, or even small-pox. If they only take twenty grammes, they will only be infected with great difficulty.

Thus it was once scientific to say that one requires so much protein as to poison oneself and be exposed to every kind of infection. That was 'science' twenty years ago! All this is a part of science; but when we see what was scientific in regard to very important matters but a short time ago, our confidence in such science is radically shaken.

This, too, is something one must bear in mind when we encounter a study like Anthroposophy that gives to our thinking, our whole mood of soul, a different direction from that customary today. I only wanted to point, so to speak, to what is put forward —in the first place—as preliminary instruction in the attainment of another kind of thinking, another way of contemplating the world.

Lecture 3

THE TRANSITION FROM ORDINARY KNOWLEDGE TO THE SCIENCE OF INITIATION

27th January, 1924

TODAY I should like to give another transitional lecture and indicate, from a certain aspect, the relation between exoteric and esoteric life; or, in other words, the transition from ordinary knowledge to knowledge attained through initiation. In this connection we must bear in mind what I have already explained in the *News Sheet for Members* when describing the Free College of Spiritual Science, namely: that the content of the Science of Initiation, expressed in appropriate words, can certainly be understood by everyone who is sufficiently free from prejudice. One should not say that a person must first be initiated himself in order to understand what the Science of Initiation has to give. Today, however, I should like to discuss the relationship of Anthroposophy to its source, which is the Science of Initiation itself. These three lectures will then form a kind of introduction to the composition of man (physical body, etheric body, etc.) which will be given next in the lectures of the General Anthroposophical Society.

When we consider the consciousness of present-day man, we are led to say: He stands here on the earth, and looks out on the wide spaces of the cosmos, but does not feel any connection between these and himself and what surrounds him on the earth. Just consider how abstractly the sun is described by all who claim today to be the representatives of sound science. Consider, too, how these same savants describe the moon. Apart from the fact that the sun warms us in summer and leaves us cold in winter, that the moon is a favourite companion of lovers under certain

39

conditions, how little thought is given to any connection between man, as he lives on earth, and the heavenly bodies.

Nevertheless, to know such connections, one need only develop a little that way of looking at things of which I spoke in the lecture before last. One need only develop a little understanding of what men once knew who stood nearer to the cosmos than we do today, who had a naïve consciousness and an instinct for knowledge rather than an intellectual knowledge, but were able to contemplate the connection between individual heavenly bodies and the life and being of man.

Now this connection between man and the heavenly bodies must enter human consciousness again. This will come about if Anthroposophy is cultivated in the right way.

Man believes today that his destiny, his 'Karma', is here on the earth, and does not look to the stars for its indications. It is for Anthroposophy to grasp man's part in the supersensible world. All that surrounds him, however, really belongs in the first place to his physical, or at most his etheric body. However far we look into the starry worlds we see the stars by their light. Now light, and all that we perceive in the world by light, is an etheric phenomenon. Thus, no matter how far we look in the universe, we do not get beyond the etheric by merely turning our gaze this way or that.

Man's being, however, reaches out into the supersensible. He carries his supersensible being from pre-earthly existence into the earthly realm, and carries it out again at death—out of the physical and the etheric too.

In reality there is in the whole of our environment on the earth or in the cosmos nothing of those worlds where man was before descending to earth and where he will be after passing through the gate of death. There are, however, two gates which lead from the physical and etheric worlds to the supersensible. One is the moon, the other the sun. We only understand the sun and moon aright when we realise that they are gates to the supersensible world, and have very much to do with what man experiences as his destiny on earth.

Consider, in the first place, the moon. The physicist knows nothing about the moon, except that it shows us reflected sunlight.

40

He knows that moonlight is reflected sunlight, and gets no further. He does not take into account that the cosmic body visible to our physical eye as the moon, was once united with our earth-existence.

The moon was once a part of the earth. In primeval times it separated off from the earth and became an individual cosmic body out there in cosmic space. That it became a separate body is not, however, the important point; after all, that can also be interpreted as a physical fact. The important point is something essentially different.

If anyone, in full earnestness, extends his studies of human civilisation and culture back into remote times, he finds a widespread primeval wisdom. From this is derived much that endures today and is really much cleverer than what our science can explore. And whoever studies, for example, the Vedas of India or the Yoga philosophy from this point of view, will feel deep reverence for what he finds. It is presented in a more poetic form to which he is not accustomed today, but it fills him with deeper reverence the more deeply he studies it. If one does not approach these things in the dry, prosaic manner of today, but lets them work upon him in their stirring, yet profound, way, one comes to understand, even from a study of the documents, that Spiritual Science, Anthroposophy, must say from its own cognition: There was once a widespread primeval wisdom, though it did not appear in an intellectual, but rather in a poetic form.

The man of today, however, is constrained by his physical body to understand, through the instrumentality of his brain, what confronts him as wisdom. Now this brain, as his instrument of understanding, has only evolved in the course of long periods of time. It did not exist when the primeval wisdom was here on earth. Wisdom was then the possession of beings who did not live in a physical body.

Such beings were once companions of men. They were the great, original teachers of humanity, who have since disappeared from the earth. It is not only the physical moon that went out into cosmic space; these beings went with it. One who looks at the moon with real insight will say: There above is a world with beings in it who once lived among us on earth, and taught us in our former earthly lives; they have retired to the colony of the moon. Only when we study things in this way do we attain to truth.

Now today, within his physical body, man is only able to contemplate a very weak infusion—if I may use this term—of the primeval wisdom. In ancient times, when these beings were his teachers, man possessed something of this wisdom. He received it, not with his understanding but with his instinct, in the way by which higher beings could reveal themselves to him.

Thus everything connected with the moon points to man's past. Now, for the man of today, the past is over and done with; he no longer possesses it. Nevertheless, he bears it within him. And though we do not, in our present condition between birth and death, really encounter those beings of whom I spoke just now who were once earth-beings but are now moon-beings, we do meet them in our pre-earthly life, in the life between death and rebirth. That which we bear within us and which is always pointing to our earlier existence before birth—which speaks from our subconscious life and never attains full intellectual clarity, but has, on this account, much to do with our feelings and emotional disposition—this directs to the moonlight, not only the instinct of lovers, but the man who can value these subconscious impulses of human nature.

Our subconscious life, then, directs us to the moon. This may witness to the fact that the moon, with the beings who dwell there, was once united with the earth. In this sense the moon is a gate to the supersensible; and one who studies it rightly will find, even in its external, physical configuration, support for this statement.

Just try to recall the way the moon, with its mountains, etc., is described. It all indicates that these mountains cannot be like those on the earth. The whole configuration of the moon is different. It is always stressed that the moon has neither air nor water, for example. The configuration of the moon is, in fact, like that of the earth before it became quite mineral.

I should have to read you a large number of my books and many passages from the lecture-cycles if I had to draw together what I am here presenting as a result of what has been worked out here. I only want to sketch, in an introductory way, how Anthroposophy proceeds. It leads us, in the manner described, from the physical to the spiritual again. Through Anthroposophy we learn to think in accordance with Nature. This men cannot do today.

For instance, men know today that the physical substance of their bodies is often changed in the course of life. We are continually 'peeling off'. We cut our nails, for example; but everything within us is moving towards the surface until, at last, what was in the centre of the body reaches the surface and peels off— You must not believe, my dear friends, that the flesh and blood— or any physical substance—sitting on your chairs today would have sat on these chairs had you been here ten years ago. That substance has all been exchanged. What has remained? Your psycho-spiritual being. Today, at least, it is known to everyone that the people sitting here today would not have had the same muscles and bones had they sat here ten or twenty years ago; only, this is not always borne in mind.

Now, when people look up at the moon, they are conscious, to a certain extent, of its external, physical substance, and believe this was the same millions of years ago. As a matter of fact, it was just as little the same then as your present physical body was the same twenty years ago. Of course, the physical substances of the stars are not exchanged so quickly; still, they do not require so long a time as our physicists estimate in the case of the sun. These calculations are absolutely accurate—but they are wrong. I have often referred to this. You see, you may measure, for example, the changes in the inner configuration of a man's heart from month to month. You may estimate them over a period of three years. You may then calculate, quite correctly, what the configuration of his heart was three hundred years ago, or what it will be in three hundred years' time. You can arrive at some fine numbers; your calculations may be quite correct—only, his heart was not there three hundred years ago, and will not be there in three hundred years to come.

Geologists calculate in this fashion today. They study the strata of the earth, estimate the changes occurring in the course of centuries, multiply their figures and say: Twenty millions of years ago the earth was so and so. This is just the same sort of calculation, and just as sensible; for twenty million years ago all these strata were not yet there, and will no longer be in twenty million years to come.

However, apart from this, all the heavenly bodies are subject to metabolism, as man is. The substances we see when we look up at the moon were just as little there a certain number of centuries ago, as your own substances were on these chairs ten years ago. It is the beings themselves who sustain the moon, just as it is the psycho-spiritual in you that maintains your body. True, the physical moon once went out into cosmic space; but what went out is continually changing its substance, while the beings who inhabit the moon remain. It is these who form the permanent element of the moon—quite apart from their passage through repeated moon-lives.—But we will not go into that today.

When you study the moon in this way you acquire a kind of 'science of the moon'. This science becomes inscribed in your heart, not merely in your head. You establish a relationship to the spiritual cosmos, and regard the moon as one gate thereto. Everything present in the depths of our being—not only the indefinite feelings of love, to mention these once again, but everything in the subconscious depths of our souls that results from earlier lives on earth—is connected with this 'moon-existence'. From this we free ourselves in all that constitutes our present life. We are continually doing so. When we see or hear outer things with our senses, when we exercise our understanding—i.e. when we disregard what comes from the depths of our soul life and is clearly recognised as part of an active past, and turn to what draws us again and again into the present—then we are directed to the 'sun-existence', just as we are directed by the past to the moon-existence. Only, the sun works on us by way of our physical bodies. If we want to acquire independently, of our own free will, what the sun gives us, we have to exert that will: we must set our intellect in action. Yet, with all that we human beings of today understand through our busy intellect and our reason, we do not get nearly so far as we do instinctively—simply through there being a sun in the universe.

Everyone knows, or can, at least, know, that the sun not only wakens us every morning, calling us from darkness to light, but is the source of the forces of growth within us, including those of the soul. That which works in these soul-forces from out of the past is connected with the moon, but that which works within the present and which we shall only really acquire in the future through our own free choice, depends on the sun.

The moon points to our past, the sun to the future. We look up to the two luminaries, that of the day and that of the night, and observe the relationship between them, for they send us the same light. Then we look into ourselves and observe all that is woven into our destiny through past experiences undergone as men; in this we see our inner moon-existence. And in all that continually approaches us in the present and determines our destiny, in all that works on from the present into the future we see the sun-element. We see how past and future are weaving together in human destiny.

Further: we can study this connection between past and future more closely. Suppose two people come together for some common task at a certain time of life. One who does not think deeply about such things may say: He and I were both at Müllheim (let us say), and we met there. He thinks no more about it. But one who thinks more deeply may follow up the lives of these two who came together when one was, perhaps, thirty years of age and the other twenty-five. He will see in what a wonderful and extraordinary way the lives of these two people have developed, step by step, from birth onwards, so as to bring them together at this place. One may say, indeed, that people find their way to one another from the most distant places to meet about half-way through their lives. It is as if they had arranged all their ways with this end in view. Of course, they could not have done this consciously, for they had not seen one another before—or, at least, had not formed such a judgment of one another as would make their meeting significant. All these things take place in the unconscious. We travel paths leading to important turning points, or periods in our lives, and do so in deep unconsciousness. It is from these depths that—in the first place—destiny is woven. (Now we begin to understand people like Goethe's friend Knebel, whose experience of life was deep and varied and who said in his old age: On looking back on my

45

life it seems as if every step had been so ordained that I had to arrive finally at a definite point.) Then the moment comes, however, when the relationship between these two people takes place in full consciousness. They learn to know one another, one another's temperament and character, they feel sympathy or antipathy for one another, etc. Now, if we examine the connection between their relationship and the cosmos, we find that moon-forces were active on the paths taken by these two people up to the moment of meeting. At this point the action of the sun begins. They now enter, to a certain extent, the bright light of the sun's activity. What follows is accompanied by their own consciousness; the future begins to illuminate the past, as the sun the moon. At the same time the past illuminates man's future, as the moon the earth with reflected light.

But the question now is, whether we can distinguish the solar from the lunar in man's life. Well, even our feelings can distinguish much, if we study them more deeply. Even in childhood and early life we come into contact with people whose relationship to us remains external; we 'pass them by' as they us, even though they may have a good deal to do with us. You all went to school, but only very few of you can say you had teachers with whom you had any deeper relationship. Still, there will be one or two of you who can say: Yes, I had a teacher who made such an impression on me that I wanted to be like him; or: He made such an impression on me that I wished him off the face of the earth. It may have been either sympathy or antipathy.

There are others, again, who only affect our understanding, so to speak, or our aesthetic sense at most. Just think how often it happens that we learn to know somebody and, meeting others who know him too, we all agree that he is a splendid fellow—or a terrible person. This is an aesthetic judgment, or an intellectual one. But there is another kind of judgment. There are human relationships that do not merely run their course in the above two ways, but affect the will; and this to such an extent that we do not merely say, as in childhood, that we would like to become like this person or that we wish him off the face of the earth—to mention extreme cases—but we are affected in the unconscious depths of our will life, and say: We not only look upon this man

46

as good or bad, clever or foolish, etc., but we would like to do, of our own accord, what his will wills; we would rather not exert our intellect in order to judge him. We would like to translate into action the impression he has made upon us.

Thus there are these two kinds of human relationships: those that affect our intellect, or, at most, our aesthetic sense; and those that affect our will, acting on the deeper life of our soul. What does that mean? Well, if people act on our will, if we do not merely feel strong sympathy or antipathy towards them but would like to give expression to our sympathy or antipathy through our will, they were somehow connected with us in our previous life. If people only impress our intellect or our aesthetic sense, they are entering our life without such a previous connection.

You can see from this that in human life, especially in human destiny, past and present work together into the future. For what we experience with others, even though they have no effect on our will, will come to expression in a future life on earth.

Just as the sun and moon circle in the same path and are interrelated, so, in the human being, are past and future, moon element and sun-element. And we can come to look upon the sun and moon, not as external luminaries, but as mirrors reflecting, in the wide spaces of the cosmos, the interweaving of our destiny. Past and future continually interpenetrate and interweave in our destinies, just as moonlight passes into sunlight, and sunlight into moonlight. Indeed, the interweaving takes place in every case of human relationship.

Consider the paths travelled by two people, the one for thirty years, the other for twenty-five. They meet here, let us say. All they have passed through until now belongs to the moon-element in man. Now, however, through learning to know one another, through confronting one another consciously, they enter the sun-element of destiny, and weave past and future together, thus forming their destiny for future lives on earth.

Thus, from the way destiny approaches man we may see how, in the one case, a person acts on another through intellect or aesthetic sense, in another case through the will and the life of feeling connected therewith.

47

As I have said, I only want today to sketch these things in a brief, fragmentary way in order to show you the path of Anthroposophy and of its source—the Science of Initiation. We shall study the details in the future. As far as I have gone at present however, everyone can have direct, first-hand knowledge of these things. He can study his destiny with understanding. That peculiar, intimate, inner relationship in which another person speaks from within us—as it were—indicates ties of destiny from the past. If I feel that someone 'grips' me, not merely in my senses and intellect but inwardly, so that my will is engaged in the very way he grips me, he is connected with me by ties of destiny from the past. Such ties can be felt with a finer, more intimate sense.

One experiences this in an essentially different way, however, when one attains a certain stage of the path described in my book *Knowledge of the Higher Worlds and its Attainment*, or in the second part of my *Occult Science*. When one attains initiation another person with whom one has ties of destiny is not only experienced in such a way that one says: He acts on my will, he acts in my will. One actually experiences the other personality as really within oneself. If an initiate meets another person with whom he has ties of destiny, this other person is present within him with independent speech and gestures—speaks from out of him, as one who stands beside us speaks to us. Thus the ties of destiny, which are usually felt only in the will, take such a form for the initiate that the other person speaks from out of the initiate himself. For one possessing the Science of Initiation a karmic encounter means, then, that the other person works not only on his will, but as strongly as a man standing beside him.

You see, what ordinary consciousness can only surmise by way of feeling and will, is raised for higher consciousness to full reality. You may say: That means that the initiate walks about with a group of people inside him with whom he is connected through destiny. That is actually the case. The attainment of knowledge is not a mere matter of learning to say more than other people while talking just as they do; it really means enlarging one's world.

Thus, if one intends to speak on the way Karma operates in

human lives, fashioning mutual destiny, one must be able to confirm what one says from a knowledge of how others speak in one, how they really become a part of oneself.

If we then describe these things, they need not remain out of reach of one who has not been initiated; for he can and—if sane and healthy—will say: True, I don't hear a person speaking within me, if we are connected through destiny; but I feel him in my will, in the way he stirs it. One learns to understand this effect on the will. One learns to understand what is experienced in ordinary consciousness but cannot be understood unless we hear it described, in its true concrete significance, out of the Science of Initiation.

It was my special concern today to explain that this feeling of karmic connection with another, which otherwise enters consciousness in a kind of nebulous way, becomes a concrete experience for the initiate. And all that the Science of Initiation can achieve, can be described in this way.

There are many other indications of our karmic connections with other people. Some of you will know, if you study life, that we meet many people of whom we do not dream; we can live long with them without doing so. We meet others, however, of whom we dream constantly. We have hardly seen them when we dream of them the next night, and they enter our dreams again and again.

Now dreams play a special part in the subconscious life. When we dream of people on first meeting them, there is certainly a karmic connection between us. People of whom we cannot dream make only a slight impression on our senses; we meet them but have no karmic connection with them.

What lives in the depths of our will is, indeed, like a waking dream; but it becomes concrete, fully conscious experience for the initiate. Hence he hears those with whom he has a karmic connection speaking from within him. Of course he remains sensible and does not walk about speaking, as an initiate, from out of others when he converses with all sorts of people. Nevertheless, he does accustom himself, under certain conditions, to hold converse with persons connected with him through Karma. This converse takes place in a quite concrete way, even when he

49

is not with them in space, and things of real significance come to light. However, I shall describe these things at some future time.

Thus we can deepen our consciousness on looking out into the wide spaces of the cosmos, and on looking into man himself. And the more we look into man himself, the more we learn to understand what the wide cosmic spaces contain. Then we say to ourselves: I no longer see merely shining discs or orbs in stellar space, but what I see in the outer cosmos appears to me as cosmically woven destiny. Human destinies on earth are now seen to be images of cosmically woven destinies. And when we realise clearly that the substance of a heavenly body is changing—is being exchanged, just as is the bodily substance of man—we know there is no sense in merely speaking of abstract laws of Nature. These abstract laws must not be regarded as giving us knowledge. It is just as in life insurance companies. To what do these owe their existence? To the fact that they can calculate a man's 'expectation of life'. One takes a certain number of people aged twenty-five and, from the number of these who reach the age of thirty, etc., one can calculate the probable number of years a man of thirty will live. He is insured accordingly. Now, one gets on quite well with such insurance, for the laws of insurance hold. But it would not occur to anyone to apply these laws to his innermost being; otherwise he would say: I insured myself at the age of thirty, because my 'probable death' would occur at the age of fifty-five. I must die at fifty-five. He would never draw this conclusion and act accordingly, although the calculation is quite correct. The correctness of the reasoning has no significance for actual life.

Now we only arrive at laws of nature by calculations. They are good for technical applications; they enable us to construct machines, just as we can insure people in accordance with certain natural laws. But they do not lead us into the true essence of things, for only real cognition of the *beings* themselves can do that.

The laws of Nature, as calculated by astronomers for the heavens, are like insurance laws in human life. What a real Science of Initiation discovers about the being of the sun or moon is like my finding someone still living in ten years' time when, according to his insurance policy, he should have died long before. It lay in his inner being to live on.

Fundamentally speaking, actual events have nothing at all to do with the laws of Nature. These laws are good, for applying natural forces; real Being, however, must be known through the Science of Initiation.

This concludes the third of the lectures in which I only wanted to indicate what the tone of Anthroposophy should be. We shall now begin to describe the constitution of man somewhat differently from the way it is done in my *Theosophy*. In doing this we shall build up an Anthroposophical Science, an Anthroposophical Knowledge from its foundations. You may regard the three lectures I have just given as illustrations of the difference in tone between the speech of ordinary consciousness and the speech of that consciousness which leads into the real being of things.

Lecture 4

'MEDITATION' AND 'INSPIRATION'

1st February, 1924

I SHALL now continue, in a certain direction, the more elementary considerations recently begun. In the first lecture of this series I drew your attention to the heart's real, inner need of finding, or at least seeking, the paths of the soul to the spiritual world. I spoke of this need meeting man from two directions: from the side of Nature, and from the side of inner experience.

Today we will again place these two aspects of human life before us in a quite elementary way. We shall then see that impulses from the subconscious are really active in all man's striving for knowledge in response to the needs of life, in his artistic aims and religious aspirations.

You can quite easily study the opposition, to which I here refer, in yourselves at any moment.

Take one quite simple fact. You are looking, let us say, at some part of your body—your hand, for example. In so far as the act of cognition itself is concerned you look at your hand exactly as at a crystal, or plant, or any other natural object. But when you look at this part of your body and go through life with this perception, you encounter that seriously disturbing fact which intrudes on all human experience and of which I spoke. You find that what you see will one day be a corpse; external Nature, on receiving it, has not the power to do anything else than destroy it. The moment man has become a corpse within the physical world and has been handed over to the elements in any form, there is no longer any possibility that the human form, which has been impressed on all the substances visible in his body, will be able to maintain itself.

All the forces of Nature which you can make the subject of any scientific study are only able to destroy man, never to build him up. Every unprejudiced study that is not guided by theory but controlled by life itself, leads us to say: We look at Nature around us in so far it is intelligible. (We will not speak, for the present, of what external cognition cannot grasp.) As civilised people of today we feel we have advanced very far indeed, for we have discovered so many laws of Nature. This talk of progress is, indeed, perfectly justified. Nevertheless, it is a fact that all these laws of Nature are, by their mode of operation, only able to destroy man, never to build him up. Human insight is unable, at first, to discover anything in the external world except laws of Nature which destroy man.

Let us now look at our inner life. We experience what we call our psychical life, i.e. our thinking, which can confront us fairly clearly, our feeling, which is less clearly experienced, and our willing, which is quite hidden from us. For, with ordinary consciousness, no one can claim insight into the way an intention —to pick up an object, let us say—works down into this very complicated organism of muscle and nerve in order to move, at length, arms and legs. What it is that here works down into the organism, between the formation of the thought and the perception of the lifted object, is hidden in complete darkness. But an indefinite impulse takes place in us, saying: I *will* this. So we ascribe will to ourselves and, on surveying our inner life, speak of thinking, feeling *and* willing.

But there is another side, and this introduces us again—in a certain sense—to what is deeply disturbing. We see that all this soul life of man is submerged whenever he sleeps and arises anew when he wakes. If we want to use a comparison we may well say: The soul life is like a flame which I kindle and extinguish again. But we see more. We see this soul life destroyed when certain organs are destroyed. Moreover, it is dependent on bodily development; being dreamlike in a little child and becoming gradually clearer and clearer, more and more awake. This increase in clarity and awareness goes hand in hand with the development of the body; and when we grow old our soul life becomes weaker again. The life of the soul thus keeps step with

53

the growth and decay of the body. We see it light up and die away.

But, however sure we may be that our soul, though dependent in its manifestations on the physical organism, has its own life, its own existence, this is not all we can say about it. It contains an element man must value above all else in life, for his whole manhood—his human dignity—depends on this. I refer to the moral element.

We cannot deduce moral laws from Nature however far we may explore it. They have to be experienced entirely within the soul; there, too, we must be able to obey them. The conflict and settlement must therefore take place entirely within the soul. And we must regard it as a kind of ideal for the moral life to be able, as human beings, to obey moral principles which are not forced upon us. Yet man cannot become an 'abstract' being only obeying *laws*. The moral life does not begin until emotions, impulses, instincts, passions, outbursts of temperament, etc., are subordinated to the settlement, reached entirely within the soul, between moral laws grasped in a purely spiritual way and the soul itself.

The moment we become truly conscious of our human dignity and feel we cannot be like beings driven by necessity, we rise to a world quite different from the world of Nature.

Now the disturbing element that, as long as there has been human evolution at all, has led men to strive beyond the life immediately visible, really springs from these two laws—however many subconscious and unconscious factors may be involved: We see, on the one hand, man's bodily being, but it belongs to Nature that can only destroy it; and, on the other hand, we are inwardly aware of ourselves as soul beings who light up and fade away, yet are bound up with what is most valuable in us—the moral element.

It can only be ascribed to a fundamental insincerity of our civilisation that people deceive themselves so terribly, turning a blind eye to this direct opposition between outer perception and inner experience. If we understand ourselves, if we refuse to be confined and constricted by the shackles which our education, with a definite aim in view, imposes upon us, if we free ourselves a little from these constraints we say at once: Man! you bear within you your soul life—your thinking, feeling and willing. All this is connected with the moral world which you must value above all else—perhaps with the religious source of all existence on which this moral world itself depends. But where is this inner life of moral adjustments when you sleep?

Of course, one can spin philosophic fantasies or fantastic philosophies about these things. One may then say: Man has a secure basis in his ego (i.e. in his ordinary ego-consciousness). The ego begins to think in St. Augustine, continues through Descartes, and attains a somewhat coquettish expression in Bergsonism today. But every sleep refutes this. For, from the moment we fall asleep to the moment of waking, a certain time elapses; and when, in the waking state, we look back on this interval of time, we do not find the ego *qua* experience. It was extinguished. And yet it is connected with what is most valuable in our lives—the moral element!

Thus we must say: Our body, whose existence we are rudely forced to admit, is certainly not a product of Nature, which has only the power to destroy and disintegrate it. On the other hand, our own soul life eludes us when we sleep, and is dependent on every rising and falling tide of our bodily life. As soon as we free ourselves a little from the constraints imposed on civilised man by his education today, we see at once that every religious or artistic aspiration—in fact, any higher striving—no matter how many subconscious and unconscious elements be involved, depends, throughout all human evolution, on these antitheses.

Of course, millions and millions of people do not realise this clearly. But is it necessary that what becomes a riddle of life for a man be clearly recognised as such? If people had to live by what they are clear about they would soon die. It is really the contributions to the general mood from unclear, subconscious depths that compose the main stream of our life. We should not say that he alone feels the riddles of life who can formulate them in an intellectually clear way and lay them before us: first riddle, second riddle, etc. Indeed, such people are the shallowest.

Someone may come who has this or that to talk over with us. Perhaps it is some quite ordinary matter. He speaks with a definite aim in view, but is not quite happy about it. He wants something, and yet does not want it; he cannot come to a decision. He is not quite happy about his own thoughts. To what is this due? It comes from the feeling of uncertainty, in the subconscious depths of his being, about the real basis of man's true being and worth. He feels life's riddles because of the polar antithesis I have described.

Thus we can find support neither in the corporeal, nor in the spiritual as we experience it. For the spiritual always reveals itself as something that lights up and dies down, and the body is recognised as coming from Nature which can, however, only destroy it.

So man stands between two riddles. He looks outwards and perceives his physical body, but this is a perpetual riddle to him. He is aware of his psycho-spiritual life, but this, too, is a perpetual riddle. But the greatest riddle is this: If I really experience a moral impulse and have to set my legs in motion to do something towards its realisation, it means—of course—I must move my body. Let us say the impulse is one of goodwill. At first this is really experienced entirely within the soul, i.e. purely psychically. How, now, does this impulse of goodwill shoot down into the body? How does a moral impulse come to move bones by muscles? Ordinary consciousness cannot comprehend this. One may regard such a discussion as theoretical, and say: We leave that to philosophers; they will think about it. Our civilisation usually leaves this question to its thinkers, and then despises—or, at least, values but little—what they say. Well; this satisfies the head only, not the heart. The human heart feels a nervous unrest and finds no joy in life, no firm foundation, no security. With the form man's thinking has taken since the first third of the fifteenth century magnificent results in the domain of external science have been achieved, but nothing has or can be contributed towards a solution of these two riddles—that of man's physical body and that of his psychical life. It is just from a clear insight into these things that Anthroposophy comes forward, saying: True; man's thinking, in the form it has so far actually taken, is powerless in the face of Reality. However much we think, we cannot in the very least influence an external process of nature by our thinking.

Moreover, we cannot, by mere thinking, influence our own 'will-organism'. To feel deeply the powerlessness of this thinking is to receive the impulse to transcend it.

But one cannot transcend it by spinning fantasies. There is no starting point but thought; you cannot begin to think about the world except by thinking. Our thinking, however, is not fitted for this. So we are unavoidably led by life itself to find—from this starting point in thought—a way by which our thinking may penetrate more deeply into existence—into Reality. This way is only to be found in what is described as meditation—for example, in my book: *Knowledge of the Higher Worlds and its Attainment*.

Today we will only describe this path in bare outline, for we intend to give the skeleton of a whole anthroposophical structure. We will begin again where we began twenty years ago.

Meditation, we may say, consists in experiencing thinking in another way than usual. Today one allows oneself to be stimulated from without; one surrenders to external reality. And in seeing, hearing, grasping, etc., one notices that the reception of external impressions is continued—to a certain extent—in thoughts. One's attitude is passive—one surrenders to the world and the thoughts come. We never get further in this way. We must begin to *experience* thinking. One does this by taking a thought that is easily comprehended, letting it stay in one's consciousness, and concentrating one's whole consciousness upon it.

Now it does not matter at all what the thought may signify for the external world. The point is simply that we concentrate our consciousness on this one thought, ignoring every other experience. I say it must be a comprehensible thought—a simple thought, that can be 'seen' from all sides [überschaubar]. A very, very learned man once asked me how one meditates. I gave him an exceedingly simple thought. I told him it did not matter whether the thought referred to any external reality. I told him to think: Wisdom is in the light. He was to apply the whole force of his soul again and again to the thought: Wisdom is in the light. Whether this be true or false is not the point. It matters just as little whether an object that I set in motion, again and again, by

57

exerting my arm, be of far-reaching importance or a game; I strengthen the muscles of my arm thereby. So, too, we strengthen our thinking when we exert ourselves, again and again, to perform the above activity, irrespective of what the thought may signify. If we strenuously endeavour, again and again, to make it present in our consciousness and concentrate our whole soul life upon it, we strengthen our soul life—just as we strengthen the muscular force of our arm if we apply it again and again to the same action. But we must choose a thought that is easily surveyed; otherwise we are exposed to all possible tricks of our own organisation. People do not believe how strong is the suggestive power of unconscious echoes of past experiences and the like. The moment we entertain a more complicated thought demonic powers approach from all sides, suggesting this or that to our consciousness. One can only be sure that one is living in one's meditation in the full awareness of normal, conscious life, if one really takes a completely surveyable thought that can contain nothing but what one is actually thinking.

If we contrive to meditate in this way, all manner of people may say we are succumbing to auto-suggestion or the like, but they will be talking nonsense. It all turns on our success in holding a 'transparent' thought—not one that works in us through subconscious impulses in some way or other. By such concentration one strengthens and intensifies his soul life—in so far as this is a life in thought. Of course, it will depend on a man's capacities, as I have often said; in the case of one man it will take a long time, in the case of another it will happen quickly. But, after a certain time, the result will be that he no longer experiences his thinking as in ordinary consciousness. In ordinary consciousness our thoughts stand there powerless; they are 'just thoughts'. But through such concentration one really comes to experience thoughts as inner being [Sein], just as one experiences the tension of a muscle—the act of reaching out to grasp an object. Thinking becomes a reality in us; we experience, on developing ourselves further and further, a *second man* within us of whom we knew nothing before.

The moment now arrives when you say to yourself: True, I am this human being who, to begin with, can look at himself externally as one looks at the things of nature; I feel inwardly, but very dimly, the tensions of my muscles, but I do not really know how my thoughts shoot down into them. But after strengthening your thinking in the way described, you feel your strengthened thinking flowing, streaming, pulsating within you; you feel the second man. This is, to begin with, an abstract characterisation. The main thing is that the moment you feel this second man within you, supra-terrestrial things begin to concern you in the way only terrestrial things did before. In this moment, when you feel your thought take on inner life—when you feel its flow as you feel the flow of your breath when you pay heed to it—you become aware of something new in your whole being. Formerly you felt for example: I am standing on my legs. The ground is below and supports me. If it were not there, if the earth did not offer me this support, I would sink into bottomless space. I am standing on something. After you have intensified your thinking and come to feel the second man within, your earthly environment begins to interest you less than before. This only holds, however, for the moments in which you give special attention to the second man. One does not become a dreamer if one advances to these stages of knowledge in a sincere and fully conscious way. One can quite easily return, with all one's wonted skill, to the world of ordinary life. One does not become a visionary and say: Oh! I have learnt to know the spiritual world; the earthly is unreal and of less value. From now on I shall only concern myself with the spiritual world. On a true, spiritual path one does not become like that, but learns to value external life more than ever when one returns to it. Apart from this, the moments in which one transcends external life in the way described and fixes attention on the second man one has discovered cannot be maintained for long. To fix one's attention in this way and with inner sincerity demands great effort, and this can only be sustained for a certain time which is usually not very long.

Now, in turning our attention to the second man, we find at the same time, that we begin to value the spatial environment of the earth as much as what is on the earth itself. We know that the crust of the earth supports us, and the various kingdoms of Nature provide the substances we must eat if our body is to receive through food the repeated stimulus it needs. We know that we are connected with terrestrial Nature in this way. We must go into the garden to pick cabbages, cook and eat them; and we know that we need what is out there in the garden and that it is connected with our 'first' or physical man. In just the same way we learn to know what the rays of the sun, the light of the moon and the twinkling of the stars around the earth are to us. Gradually we attain one possible way of thinking of the spatial environment of the earth in relation to our 'second man', as we formerly thought of our first (physical) body in relation to its physical environment.

And now we say to ourselves: What you bear within you as muscles, bones, lung, liver, etc., is connected with the cabbage, the pheasant, etc., out there in the world. But the 'second man' of whom you have become conscious through strengthening your thinking, is connected with the sun and the moon and all the twinkling stars—with the spatial environment of the earth. We become more familiar with this environment than we usually are with our terrestrial environment—unless we happen to be food-specialists. We really gain a second world which, to begin with, is spatial.

We learn to esteem ourselves inhabitants of the world of stars as we formerly considered ourselves inhabitants of the earth. Hitherto we did not realise that we dwell in the world of stars; for a science which does not go as far to strengthen man's thinking cannot make him conscious of his connection, through a second man, with the spatial environment of the earth—a connection similar to that between his physical body and the physical earth. Such a science does not know this. It engages in calculations; but even the calculations of Astrophysics, etc., only reveal things which do not really concern man at all, or—at most—only satisfy his curiosity. After all, what does it mean to a man, or his inner life, to know how the spiral nebular in *Canes venatici* may be thought of as having originated, or as still evolving? Moreover, it is not even true! Such things do not really concern us. Man's attitude towards the world of stars is like that of some disembodied spirit towards the earth—if such a spirit be thought of as coming from some region or other to visit the earth, requiring neither ground to stand on, nor nourishment, etc. But, in actual fact, from a mere citizen of the earth man becomes a citizen of the universe when he strengthens his thinking in the above way.

We now become conscious of something quite definite, which can be described in the following way. We say to ourselves: It is good that there are cabbages, corn, etc., out there; they build up our physical body (if I may use this somewhat incorrect expression in accordance with the general, but very superficial, view). I am able to discover a certain connection between my physical body and what is there outside in the various kingdoms of Nature. But with strengthened thinking I begin to discover a similar connection between the 'second man' who lives in me and what surrounds me in supra-terrestrial space. At length one comes to say: If I go out at night and only use my ordinary eyes, I see nothing; by day the sunlight from beyond the earth makes all objects visible. To begin with, I know nothing. If I restrict myself to the earth alone, I know: there is a cabbage, there a quartz crystal. I see both by the light of the sun, but on earth I am only interested in the difference between them.

But now I begin to know that I myself, as the second man, am made of that which makes cabbage and crystal visible. It is a most significant leap in consciousness that one takes here—a complete metamorphosis. From this point one says to oneself: If you stand on the earth you see what is physical and connected with your physical man. If you strengthen your thinking the supra-terrestrial spatial world begins to concern you and the second man you have discovered—just as the earthly, physical world concerned you before. And, as you ascribe the origin of your physical body to the physical earth, you now ascribe your 'second existence' to the cosmic ether through whose activities earthly things become visible. From your own experience you can now speak of having a physical body *and an etheric body*. You see, merely to systematise and think of man as composed of various members gives no real knowledge. We only attain real insight into these things by regarding the complete metamorphosis of consciousness that results from really discovering such a second man within.

I stretch out my physical arm and my physical hand takes hold of an object. I feel, in a sense, the flowing force in this action.

Through strengthening my thought I come to feel that it is inwardly mobile and now induces a kind of 'touching' within me—a touching that also takes place in an organism; this is the etheric organism; that finer, supersensible organism which exists no less than the physical organism, though it is connected with the supra-terrestrial, not the terrestrial.

The moment now arrives when one is obliged to descend another step, if I may put it so. Through such 'imaginative' thinking as I have described we come, at first, to feel this inward touching of the second man within us; we come, too, to see this in connection with the far spaces of the universal ether. By this term you are to understand nothing but what I have just spoken of; do not read into it a meaning from some other quarter. Now, however, we must return again to ordinary consciousness if we are to get further.

You see, if we are thinking of man's physical body in the way described, we readily ask how it is really related to its environment. It is doubtless related to our physical, terrestrial environment; but how?

If we take a corpse, which is, indeed, a faithful representation of physical man—even of the living physical man—we see, in sharp contours, liver, spleen, kidney, heart, lung, bones, muscles and nerve strands. These can be drawn; they have sharp contours and resemble in this everything that occurs in solid forms. Yet there is a curious thing about this sharply outlined part of the human organism. Strictly speaking, there is nothing more deceptive than our handbooks of anatomy or physiology, for they lead people to think: there is a liver, there a heart, etc. They see all this in sharp contours and imagine this sharpness to be essential. The human organism is looked upon as a conglomeration of solid things. But it is not so at all. Ten per cent., at most, is solid; the other ninety per cent. is fluid or even gaseous. At least ninety per cent. of man, while he lives, is a column of water.

Thus we can say: In his physical body man belongs, it is true, to the solid earth—to what the ancient thinkers in particular called the 'earth'. Then we come to what is fluid in man; and even in external science one will never gain a reasonable idea of man until one learns to distinguish the solid man from the fluid man—

this inner surging and weaving element which really resembles a small ocean.

But what is terrestrial can only really affect man through the solid part of him. For even in external Nature you can see, where the fluid element begins, an inner formative force working with very great uniformity. Take the whole fluid element of our earth —its water; it is a great drop. Wherever water is free to take its own form, it takes that of a drop. The fluid element tends everywhere to be drop-like.

What is earthly—or solid, as we say today—occurs in definite, individual forms, which we can recognise. What is fluid, however, tends always to take on spherical form.

Why is this? Well, if you study a drop, be it small or as large as the earth itself, you find it is an image of the whole universe. Of course, this is wrong according to the ordinary conceptions of today; nevertheless it appears so, to begin with, and we shall soon see that this appearance is justified. The universe really appears to us as a hollow sphere into which we look.

Every drop, whether small or large, appears as a reflection of the universe itself. Whether you take a drop of rain, or the waters of the earth as a whole, the surface gives you a picture of the universe. Thus, as soon as you come to what is fluid, you cannot explain it by earthly forces. If you study closely the enormous efforts that have been made to explain the spherical form of the oceans by terrestrial forces, you will realise how vain such efforts are. The spherical form of the oceans cannot be explained by terrestrial gravitational attraction and the like, but by pressure from without. Here, even in external Nature, we find we must look beyond the terrestrial. And, in doing this, we come to grasp how it is with man himself.

As long as you restrict yourself to the solid part of man, you need not look beyond the terrestrial in understanding his form. The moment you come to his fluid part, you require the *second man* discovered by strengthened thinking. He works in what is fluid.

We are now back again at what is terrestrial. We find in man a solid constituent; this we can explain with our ordinary thoughts. But we cannot understand the form of his fluid components

63

unless we think of the second man as active within him—the second man whom we contact within ourselves in our strengthened thinking as the human etheric body.

Thus we can say: The physical man works in what is solid, the etheric man in what is fluid. Of course, the etheric man still remains an independent entity, but he works through the fluid medium.

We must now proceed further. Imagine we have actually got so far as to experience inwardly this strengthened thinking and, therefore, the etheric—the second—man. This means, that we are developing great inner force. Now, as you know, one can—with a little effort—not only let oneself be stimulated to think, but can even refrain from all thinking. One can stop thinking; and our physical organisation does this for us when we are tired and fall asleep. But it becomes more difficult to extinguish again, of our own accord, the strengthened thinking which results from meditation and which we have acquired by great effort. It is comparatively easy to extinguish an ordinary, powerless thought; to put away—or 'suggest away'—the strengthened thinking one has developed demands a stronger force, for one cleaves in a more inward way to what one has thus acquired. If we succeed, however, something special occurs.

You see, our ordinary thinking is stimulated by our environment, or memories of our environment. When you follow a train of thought the world is still there; when you fall asleep the world is still there. But it is out of this very world of visible things that you have raised yourself in your strengthened thinking. You have contacted the supra-terrestrial spatial environment, and now study your relationship to the stars as you formerly studied the relation between the natural objects around you. You have now brought yourself into relation with all this, but can suppress it again. In suppressing it, however, the external world, too, is no longer there—for you have just directed all your interest to this strengthened consciousness. The outer world is not there; and you come to what one can call 'empty consciousness'. Ordinary consciousness only knows emptiness in sleep, and then in the form of unconsciousness.

What one now attains is just this: one remains fully awake,

receiving no outer sense impressions, yet not sleeping—merely 'waking'. Yet one does not remain merely awake. For now, on exposing one's empty consciousness to the indefinite on all sides, the spiritual world proper enters. One says: the spiritual world approaches me. Whereas previously one only looked out into the supra-terrestrial physical environment—which is really an etheric environment—and saw what is spatial, something new, the actual spiritual world, now approaches through this cosmic space from all sides as from indefinite distances. At first the spiritual approaches you from the outermost part of the cosmos when you traverse the path I have described.

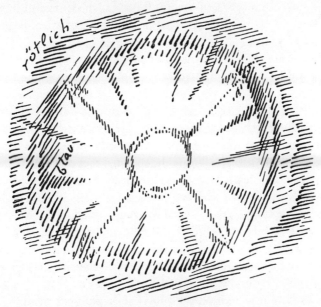

(*rötlich*—reddish; *blau*—blue)

A third thing is now added to the former metamorphosis of consciousness. One now says: I bear with me my physical body (inner circle), my etheric body (blue) which I apprehended in my strengthened thinking, and something more that comes from the undefined—from beyond space. I ask you to notice that I am talking of the world of appearance; we shall see in the course of the next few days how far one is justified in speaking of the etheric as coming from the spatial world, and of what lies beyond us (red) coming from the Undefined. We are no longer conscious of this third component as coming from the spatial world. It streams to us through the cosmic ether and permeates us as a 'third man'. We have now a right to speak, from our own experience, of a first or physical man, a second or etheric man, and a third or 'astral man'. (You realise, of course, that you must not be put off by words.) We bear within us an astral or third man, who comes from the spiritual, not merely from the etheric. We can speak of the astral body or astral man.

Now we can go further. I will only indicate this in conclusion so that I can elaborate it tomorrow. We now say to ourselves: I breathe in, use my breath for my inner organisation and breathe out. But is it really true that what people think of as a mixture of oxygen and nitrogen enters and leaves us in breathing?

Well, according to the views of present day civilisation, what enters and leaves is composed of oxygen and nitrogen and some other things. But one who attains 'empty consciousness' and then experiences this onrush—as I might call it—of the spiritual through the ether, experiences in the breath he draws something not formed out of the ether alone, but out of the spiritual beyond it. He gradually learns to know the spiritual that plays into man in respiration. He learns to say to himself: You have a physical body; this works into what is solid—that is its medium. You have your etheric body; this works into what is fluid. But, in being a man—not merely a solid man or fluid man, but a man who bears his 'air man' within him—your third or astral man can work into what is airy or gaseous. It is through this material substance on the earth that your astral man operates.

Man's fluid organisation with its regular but ever changing life will never be grasped by ordinary thinking. It can only be grasped by strengthened thinking. With ordinary thinking we can only apprehend the definite contours of the physical man. And, since our anatomy and physiology merely take account of the body, they only describe ten per cent. of man. But the 'fluid man' is in constant movement and never presents a fixed contour. At one moment it is like this, at another, like that—now long, now short. What is in constant movement cannot be grasped with the closed concepts suitable for calculations; you require concepts mobile in

66

themselves—'pictures'. The etheric man within the fluid man is apprehended in pictures.

The third or astral man who works in the 'airy' man, is apprehended not merely in pictures but in yet another way. If you advance further and further in meditation—I am here describing the Western process—you notice, after reaching a certain stage in your exercises, that your breath has become something palpably musical. You experience it as inner music; you feel as if inner music were weaving and surging through you. The third man— who is physically the airy man, spiritually the astral man—is experienced as an inner musical element. In this way you take hold of your breathing.

The oriental meditator did this directly by concentrating on his breathing, making it irregular in order to experience how it lives and weaves in man. He strove to take hold of this third man directly.

Thus we discover the nature of the third man, and are now at the stage when we can say: By deepening and strengthening our insight we learn, at first, to distinguish in man:

(1) the physical body which lives in solid forms on the earth and is also connected with the terrestrial kingdoms,
(2) the fluid man in whom an ever mobile, etheric element lives and which can only be apprehended in images (Bilder) —in moving, plastic images,
(3) the astral man who has his physical copy or image (Abbild) in all that constitutes the stream of inspired air.

This stream enters and takes hold of our inner organisation, expands, works, is transformed and streams out again. That is a wonderful process of becoming. We cannot draw it; we might do so symbolically, at most, but not as it really is. You could no more draw this process than you could draw the tones of a violin. You might do this symbolically; nevertheless you must direct your musical sense to *hearing inwardly*—i.e. you must attend with your inner, musical ear and not merely listen to the external tones. In this inward way you must hear the weaving of your breath—must hear the human astral body. This is the third man.

67

We apprehend him when we attain to 'empty consciousness' and allow this to be filled with 'inspirations' from without.

Now language is really cleverer than men, for it comes to us from primeval worlds. There is a deep reason why breathing was once called inspiration. In general, the words of our language say much more than we, in our abstract consciousness, feel them to contain.

These are the considerations that can lead us to the three members of man—the physical, the etheric and the astral bodies—which find expression in the solid, fluid and airy 'men' and have their physical counterparts in the forms of the solid man, in the changing shapes of the fluid man and in that which permeates man as an inner music, experienced through feeling. The nervous system is indeed the most beautiful representation of this inner music. It is built from out of the astral body—from out of this inner music; and for this reason it has, at a definite part, the wonderful configuration of the spinal cord with its attached nerve-strands. All this together is a wonderful, musical structure that is continually working upwards into man's head.

A primeval wisdom that was still alive in Ancient Greece, felt the presence of this wonderful instrument in man. For the air assimilated through breathing ascends through the whole spinal cord. The air we breathe in 'enters' the cerebro-spinal canal and pulsates upwards towards the brain. This music is actually performed, but it remains unconscious; only the upper rebound is in consciousness. This is the lyre of Apollo, the inner musical instrument that the instinctive, primeval wisdom still recognised in man. I have referred to these things before, but it is my present intention to give a résumé of what has been developed within our society in the course of twenty-one years.

Tomorrow I shall go further and consider the fourth member of man, the ego organisation proper. I shall then show the connection between these various members of man and his life on earth and beyond it—i.e. his so-called eternal life.

Lecture 5

LOVE, INTUITION AND THE HUMAN EGO

2nd February, 1924

I HAVE described how man must be regarded as composed of physical, etheric and astral bodies, and how we can acquire a deeper insight into this composition by exercising our cognitive powers—powers of mind, heart and will—in a certain way. This composition that we discern in man is also found in the external world. Only, we must be clear that there is a considerable difference between what we find in the world outside and what we find in man.

When, to begin with, we study the physical world—and we can really only study its solid, 'earthy' manifestations—we come to distinguish various substances. I need not go into details. You know, of course, that the anatomist, investigating what remains of the living man after he has passed through the gate of death—the corpse—need not take account of any but earthly substances which he also finds outside man. At least, he believes he need not, and within certain limits his belief is justified. He investigates the elements or the salts, acids and other compounds found outside of man, and he investigates what the human organism contains. He does not find it necessary to enlarge his physical and chemical knowledge.

Indeed, the difference only becomes apparent when we study these things on a somewhat bigger scale, and notice what I have emphasised so strongly, namely: that the human organism as a whole cannot be maintained by external Nature, but is subject to destruction. Thus we can say that, in the solid, earthy, physical realm, we do not find, to begin with, very much difference between what is outside and what is inside man. We must

69

recognise a greater difference however, in what is etheric.

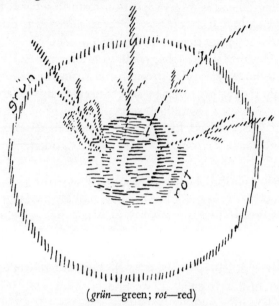

(*grün*—green; *rot*—red)

I have drawn your attention to the way the etheric really looks
down on us from the world beyond the earth. I pointed out that,
from out of the etheric, everything, whether it be a large or small
drop, is made spherical, and that this tendency to spherical
formation, due to the complex of etheric forces, extends to the
etheric body of man. We have really to fight continually to
overcome this tendency in our etheric body.—Of course, all this
takes place in the subconscious. In its present form the human
etheric body is closely moulded to the physical body. It has not
such sharp boundaries and is mobile in itself; nevertheless we can
distinguish a head part, a trunk part and, indistinctly, limb parts
where the etheric body becomes diffuse. Thus, when we move an
arm the etheric body, which otherwise conforms to the human
shape, only protrudes a little beyond the arm, whereas below it
is widely extended. But it has from the cosmos the tendency to
take on spherical form. The higher being of man—the astral man
and the ego—must oppose this tendency and mould the spherical
form to the human shape. So we may say: man, as an etheric
being, lives in the general etheric world by building up his own

70

form out of the etheric, whereas the formative tendency of the surrounding etheric is to give spherical form to what is fluid. In man what is fluid takes on human form, and this is due to his inner forces opposing the external, cosmic forces.

This opposition is still stronger in the astral man. As I indicated yesterday, the astral comes streaming in from the indefinite, so to speak. In the earthly realm outside man it streams in (arrows in green circle) in such a way that it develops the plant form out of the earth; and the plant form clearly shows this response to the astral. The plant has only an etheric body, but it is, indeed, the astral forces which draw the plant out of the earth. Now the human astral body is extraordinarily complicated and one really perceives it in the way I described yesterday, i.e. as an inner musical element, a whirling, weaving life, an inner activity and all one might describe as music inwardly sensed. But everything else that is astral is discovered streaming in centripetally; it is transformed into the human astral form, whereby complicated things appear.

Let us say, for example, that something astral is streaming in from this side. The human being moulds it to the most varied forms in order to make it serviceable and incorporate it. One might say, the human being wins his astral body by subduing the centripetal astral forces.

Now, when we turn our psycho-spiritually sharpened gaze to the cosmos, we do gain the conception of the etheric as described, but we also receive the impression that it is due to the etheric that we strive away from the earth. While we are held to the earth by gravity, we tend away from the earth because of the etheric. It is really the etheric that is active in this centrifugal tendency. In this connection you need only think of the following: The human brain weighs approximately 1,500 grammes. Now a mass with this weight, pressing on the delicate blood vessels at the base of the brain, would quite compress them. If our brain actually exerted its 1,500 grammes weight in the living man we could not have these blood-vessels. In the living man, however, the brain weighs twenty grammes at most. It is so much lighter because it floats in the cerebral fluid and loses in weight by the weight of fluid displaced. The brain really strives away from man; and in this tendency the etheric is active. Thus we may say that it is just in the brain that we can see most clearlv how matters stand.

Here is the brain floating in its fluid, whereby its weight is reduced from 1,500 to about twenty grammes. This means that its activity shares, to a remarkably small degree, in our physical, bodily life. Here the etheric finds tremendous scope for acting upwards. The weight acts downwards but is reduced. In the cerebral fluid there is principally developed the sum of etheric forces that lifts us away from the earth. Indeed, if we had to carry our physical body with all its forces of weight, we would have a sack to drag about. Every blood corpuscle, however, swims and is reduced in weight.

This loss of weight in a fluid is an old piece of knowledge. You know, of course, that it has been ascribed to Archimedes. He was bathing one day and noticed, on lifting his leg out of the water, how much heavier it was than when in the water, and exclaimed: Eureka! I have found it. He had discovered that every body in a fluid loses in weight the weight of the fluid displaced. Thus, if you think of Archimedes in his bath, here his physical leg and here the same leg formed of water, then the physical leg is lighter in water by the amount that this water-leg weighs. It is lighter by just this amount. Likewise the weight of our brain in the cerebral fluid is reduced by the weight of a mass of cerebral fluid of the size of the physical brain. That is, it is reduced from 1,500 to 20 grammes. In physics this is called 'upthrust', and here the etheric acts. The astral, on the other hand, is stimulated—to begin with—by breathing, whereby the airy element enters the human organism and eventually reaches the head in an extremely attenuated state; in this distribution and organisation of the air the astral is active.

Thus we can really see in the solid earthy substance the physical; in the fluid, especially in the way it works in man, the etheric; in the airy, the astral.

It is the tragedy of materialism that it knows nothing of matter—how matter actually works in the several domains of life. The remarkable thing about materialism is just its ignorance of matter. It knows nothing at all about the way matter works, for one does not learn this until one is able to attend to the spiritual that is active in matter and is represented by the forces.

Now, when one progresses through meditation to the 'imaginative' knowledge of which I have already spoken, one finds the etheric at work in all the aqueous processes of the earth. In the face of real knowledge it is childish to believe that all that is at work here—in the sea, in the rivers, rising mists, falling drops and cloud formations—contains only what the physicist and chemist know about water. For in all that is out there in the mighty drop of the 'water-earth', in what constantly rises in the form of vapour, forms clouds and descends as mist, in all the other aqueous processes—water plays, indeed, an enormous part in shaping the face of the globe—in all this etheric currents are working. Here is weaving the ether revealed to one in 'pictures' when one has strengthened one's thinking in the way I have described. Everywhere behind this weaving water the cosmic 'imagination' is weaving, and the astral 'music of the spheres' plays everywhere into this cosmic imagination, coming—in a sense— from behind.

In man, however, all these conditions are found to be quite different from what they are outside him. If one looks, with vision sharpened in the way I have indicated, at what is outside man, one finds the world built up in the following way: To begin with, there is the physical, in direct contact with the earth; the etheric, which fills the whole cosmos; then the astral, which streams in as living beings. Indeed, it is no merely general, abstract, astral weaving that we behold, but actual beings entering space, beings of a psycho-spiritual nature—just as man, in his body, is also a psycho-spiritual being. This is what one beholds.

If we now look back to man, we find in him, too, an etheric body corresponding to the external etheric. But this etheric body is not perceived in such a way that you can say: there is the physical man, and here is his etheric body. Certainly, you can draw it so, but that would only be an arrested section. You never see merely the present etheric body; this section which you can draw is seen to be continuous with what has gone before. You always see the whole etheric body extending back to birth. Past and present form a whole. If you have a twenty-year-old person

73

before you, you cannot see merely his twenty-year-old etheric body; you see all that has happened in his etheric body back to birth and a little beyond. Here time really becomes space. It is just as when you look down an avenue and see the trees drawing closer and closer together on account of perspective; you see the whole avenue *in space*. Likewise you look at the etheric body as it is at present but see its whole structure, which is a 'time-structure'. The etheric body is a 'time-organism', the physical body a 'space-organism'. The physical body is, of course, self-contained at any given moment; the etheric body is always there as a totality which comprises our life up to the given moment. This is a unity. Hence you could only draw or paint the etheric body if you could paint moving pictures; but you would have to be quicker than the pictures. The momentary configuration that you draw or paint is only a section and is related to the whole etheric body as the section of a tree-stem to the whole tree. When you draw a diagram of the etheric body, it is only a section, for the whole etheric body is a 'time-process'. Indeed, on surveying this time-process one is led beyond birth, even beyond conception, to the point where one sees the human being descend from his pre-earthly life to his present life on earth, and, just before he was conceived by his parents, draw together etheric substance from the general cosmic ether to build his etheric body.

Thus you cannot speak of the etheric body without surveying man's life in time back to birth and beyond. What one regards as the etheric body at some definite moment is only an abstraction; the concrete reality is the time-process.

It is different again with the astral body. This is apprehended in the way I described yesterday. I can only draw it diagramatically, and in the diagram space must become time for you. Let us assume we are observing the astral body of a person on the 2nd February 1924. Let this be the person.* He does indeed make this impression upon us: Here is the physical body, here his etheric body. We can also observe his astral body and this makes upon us the impression I described in my book *Theosophy*. It is so. But when one comes to the really 'inspired' knowledge which appears before empty consciousness—I described such knowledge

* A sketch—not reproduced—was made.

yesterday—one attains the following insight. One says to oneself: What I am observing as the astral body of this person is not really present today, i.e. on the 2nd February 1924. If the person is twenty years of age, you must go backwards in time—let us say, to January 1904. You perceive that this astral body is really back there, and extends still further back into the unlimited. It has remained there and has not accompanied him through life. Here we have only a kind of appearance—a beam. It is like looking down an avenue; there, in the distance, are the last trees, very close together. Behind them is a source of light. You can have the radiance of the light *here*, but the source is behind—it need not move forward that its light may shine here.

So, too, the astral body has remained behind, and only throws its beam into life. It has really remained in the spiritual world and has not come with us into the physical. In respect to our astral body we always remain before conception and birth, in the spiritual world. If we are twenty years old in 1924, it is as if we were still living spiritually before the year 1904 and, in respect to our astral body, had only stretched forth a feeler.

That, you will say, is a difficult conception. Well, so it is. But you know there was once a Spanish king who was shown how complicated the structure of the universe is. He thought he would have made it simpler. A man may think like this, but, as a matter of fact, the world is not simple, and we must exert ourselves somewhat to grasp what man is.

To look intently at the astral body is to look directly into the spiritual world. (Only in the world external to man have you around you what is astral.) When you look at human beings spiritually, you look into the spiritual world in respect to their astral bodies. You perceive directly what a man has undergone in the spiritual world before he descended to earth.

But, you will say, my astral body is active within me. Of course it is; that is self-understood. But imagine some being or other were here, and by means of cords mechanically connected, were to produce some effect at a considerable distance away. It is like that with respect to time. Your astral body has remained behind, but its activities extend through the whole of your life. Thus the activity that you notice in your astral body today has its origin in a time long past, when you were in the spiritual world before descending to earth. That time is still active—in other words, it is still there, as far as the spiritual is concerned. Anyone who believes that the past is no longer 'present' in the real time-process resembles a man in a railway train to whom one might say: That was a beautiful district through which we have just passed, and who would reply: Yes, a beautiful district. But it has vanished; it is no longer there. Such a man would believe that the district through which he had passed in an express train had disappeared. It is just as stupid to believe that the past is no longer there. As a matter of fact it is always there, working into man. The 3rd of January 1904, is still there in its spiritual constitution, just as what is spatial remains after you have travelled through it. It is there, influencing the present.

Thus, if you describe the astral body as I have done in my *Theosophy*, you must realise, in order to complete your insight, that what is active here is the 'radiance' of something far back in time. The human being is really like a comet stretching its tail far back into the past. It is not possible to obtain true insight into man's being unless we acquire these new concepts.

People who believe one can enter the spiritual world with the same concepts one has for the physical world should become spiritualists, not anthroposophists. Spiritualists endeavour to conjure the spiritual—only somewhat thinner than ordinary matter—into the ordinary space in which physical men walk about. But it is nothing spiritual—only fine exudations. Even the phantoms described by Schrenk-Notzing are only fine, physical exudations which retain in their shape traces of the etheric. They are mere phantoms, not something really spiritual.

If you study the world and man in the way I have described you will realise the presence of the higher worlds in external Nature. In the case of man, a study of the successive worlds will lead you at once to the 'time-process' within him. In his case, however, you can go further still and reach a domain which our philistine materialistic age will not recognise as accessible to knowledge.

I have referred to perception, by the senses, of the coarse, tangible physical objects around us as the first stage of cognition.

The second stage was that of 'strengthened thinking' in which we apprehend the living, moving images of the world. The third kind of cognition was 'inspiration' in which we perceive the beings that express themselves through these images—hear a kind of music of the spheres that sounds from beyond. In the case of man we are led, not merely out of the material world, but out of the present into his pre-earthly life—into his existence as a psycho-spiritual being before descending to earth. This 'inspired' knowledge is attained by emptying our consciousness *after* strengthened thinking.

The further stage in cognition is attained by making the power of love a cognitive force. Only, it must not be the shallow love of which alone, as a rule, our materialistic age speaks. It must be the love by which you can identify yourself with another being— a being with whom, in the physical world, you are not identical. You must really be able to feel what is passing in the other being just as you feel what is passing in yourself; you must be able to go out of yourself and live again in another. In ordinary human life such love does not attain the intensity necessary to make it a cognitive force. One must first have attained 'empty consciousness', and have had some experience with it. And then we undergo what many who are striving for higher knowledge do not seek: we suffer what may be called the *pain of knowledge*.

If you have a wound somewhere, it hurts you. Why? Because, owing to the wound, your spiritual being cannot permeate your physical body properly at the place concerned. All pain comes from not being able, from one cause or another, to permeate the physical body. And when something external hurts you, this is also because you are unable to 'unite' yourself with it—to accept it. Now, when one has attained the empty consciousness into which there flows an altogether different world from that to which one is accustomed, then, for such moments of inspired cognition, one is without one's whole physical man; this is then one large wound and hurts all over. One must first undergo this experience; one must endure the leaving of the physical body as actual pain and suffering in order to attain inspired knowledge. Of course, an understanding of such knowledge can be acquired without pain, and people should acquire this understanding apart from suffering the pain of initiation. But to acquire an immediate, spiritual perception—not a mere understanding—of what works into man from his life before birth, that is, of what he leaves behind in the spiritual world, one must cross the abyss of universal suffering and pain.

We can then experience the above identification with, and coming to life in, another being. Only then do we learn the highest degree of love which consists not in 'forgetting oneself' in a theoretical sense, but in being able to ignore oneself completely and enter into what is not oneself. And only when this love goes hand in hand with that higher—inspired—cognition are we really able to enter the spiritual with all the warmth of our nature, with all our inwardness of heart and mind; that is, with our *soul* forces. We must do this if we are to progress in knowledge. Love must become a cognitive force in this sense. When such love has attained a certain height and intensity, you pass through your pre-earthly life to your last life on earth; you slip over, through all you have undergone between your last death and your present life, into your former life on earth—into what we call previous incarnations.

Now, it was, of course, also in a physical body that you then trod the earth. But nothing remains of all that made up that physical body; it has been absorbed into the elements. Your innermost being of that time has become entirely spiritual and lives in you as spirit alone.

In truth, our ego, in passing through the gate of death and the spiritual world to a new life on earth, becomes wholly spiritual. It cannot be grasped with the ordinary powers of every-day consciousness; we must intensify the power of love in the way I have described. The man we were in a previous life is just as much outside us as another human being of today. Our ego has the same degree of externality. Of course, we then come to possess it—to experience it as ourself—but we must first learn to love without any trace of egotism. It would be a terrible thing indeed, if we were to become enamoured—in the ordinary sense—of our former incarnation. Love, in the highest sense, must be intensified so that we may be able to experience our former incarnation as something quite other than ourself. Then, when our cognitive power emerges through the empty consciousness, we acquire knowledge through love intensified in the highest degree, and reach the fourth member of man—the ego proper.

Man has his physical body through which he lives at each moment in the *present* physical earth. He has his etheric body through which he lives continually in a time-process extending back to a little before his birth, when he drew together this etheric body out of the general cosmic ether. He has his astral body through which his life extends over the whole period between his last death and his last descent to earth. And he has his ego through which he reaches back into his previous life on earth. Thus, when we speak of the various members of man's being we must speak, in each case, of his extension in time. We bear our former ego-consciousness within us today, but unconsciously. How? If you want to study how you must realise that man, here in the physical world, is not only a solid body, a fluid man and an airy man, but an organism of warmth as well. This is also the way to approach the ego. Everyone knows this, at least in a very partial way. If we measure a person's temperature we get different degrees of fever in different parts of the body. But there are different temperatures throughout man's whole organism. You have one temperature in your head, another in your big toe, another inside your liver, another within your lung. You are not only what you find drawn in definite outlines in an anatomical atlas. You have a fluid organism in constant motion. You have an organism of air which permeates you continually, like a mighty, symphonic organism of music. And, in addition, you have a surging organism of warmth, differentiated with respect to temperature. In this you yourself live. Indeed, you feel that this is so. After all, you are not very conscious of living in your shin-bone, or in any other bone, or in your liver, or in your vascular fluids. But you are very conscious of living in your warmth, though you do not distinguish between your 'warmth-hand', 'warmth-leg', 'warmth-liver', etc. Nevertheless this differentiation is there, and if the temperature differences proper to the human warmth-organism are absent or disturbed, we feel this as illness, as pain.

When, with developed consciousness, we attain the picture

stage—'imagination'—we perceive the etheric as weaving pictures. When we perceive the astral, we hear the music of the spheres which sounds towards us or, we might say, from out of ourselves. (For our own astral body leads us back to our pre-earthly life.) And when we advance farther to the form of cognition that attains the highest degree of love—when the power of love becomes a cognitive force—when, to begin with, we see our own existence flowing from a former life on earth into this present life, we feel this former life in the normal differentiation of the 'warmth-organism' in which we are living. This is real intuition. We live in this. And when some impulse arises in us to do this or that, it does not only work, as in the astral body, out of the spiritual world, but from still farther back—from our former life on earth. Our former life on earth works into the warmth of our organism, and kindles this or that impulse. Thus we see in the earthly, solid man the physical body, in the fluid man the etheric body, in the airy man the astral body, and in the warmth element the ego proper. (The ego of the present incarnation is never complete; it is always developing.) It is the ego of the former life on earth, working in subconscious depths, that is the ego proper. And when you perceive a man clairvoyantly you are led to say: He is standing here and I see him, to begin with, with my external senses. But I also see what is etheric and what is astral; then, behind him, the man he was in his previous incarnation.

In fact, the more this consciousness is developed, the more clearly do we see, in a kind of perspective, the head of his last incarnation a little above the head of his present incarnation, and, somewhat higher still, the head of his second last incarnation. In civilisations in which there was still a kind of instinctive consciousness of these things, you will find pictures which show, behind the clearly drawn countenance of the present incarnation, a second countenance less clearly painted; behind this a third that is still

80

less clear. There are Egyptian pictures like this. You understand such pictures if you are able to perceive, behind the present man, the man he was in his last and second last incarnations. Not until one can extend man's life in time to include previous incarnations can one really speak of the ego as the fourth member of human nature.

All this acts in the 'man of warmth'. 'Inspiration' approaches you from without or from within, you yourself are within the warmth; here is 'intuition', true intuition. We experience warmth within us quite differently from anything else.

Now, if you look at it in this way, you will get beyond what should be a great riddle to the man of today, if he gives attention to his soul in a really unprejudiced way. I have spoken of this riddle. I said, we feel ourselves morally determined by certain impulses given us in a purely spiritual way. We want to carry them out. But we cannot, to begin with, understand how that to which we feel ourselves morally bound shoots into our muscles. If, however, we know that we bear within us, from our last incarnation, our ego which has become entirely spiritual and now acts upon our warmth-man, we have the required connection. Our moral impulses act indirectly, through the ego of our last incarnation. Here the connection between the moral and the physical is first found. It cannot be found by merely studying the present world of Nature and man as a section of it.

You see, if you study the present world of Nature, you may say: Well, there outside is Nature; man takes in its substances and builds up his organism—one does actually picture it in this naïve way. Thus man is a portion of Nature, being compounded of certain of its substances. Good! But you suddenly realise that there are moral impulses and you should act in accordance with them! How, I would ask, can a portion of Nature do that? A stone cannot do it, nor can calcium, or chlorine, or oxygen, or nitrogen. But man, who is compounded of these, is supposed to be able to do so! He experiences a moral impulse and is expected to act in accordance with it, although he is compounded of all these substance which cannot do so.

But in all that is thus welded together in man there arises—especially indirectly through sleep—something that passes through

81

death, becomes more and more spiritual, and enters a body again. It is, of course, already in the present body, for it comes from the last incarnation. It became spiritual and now works into the present incarnation. What is compounded of earthly substances will work into the warmth-man of the next incarnation. Here the moral element flows from one earth life into another; here we can grasp the transition from physical to spiritual Nature and from spiritual to physical Nature again. We cannot understand this transition with one life alone, if we are honest with ourselves and do not close our eyes to the whole psycho-spiritual problem.

What we can regard as the earthly elements—the solid, liquid, gaseous and warmth elements—is permeated everywhere by what can be designated as the etheric, the astral and the 'ego-like', i.e. what is of like nature with the ego. In this way we see the connection between man's members and the universe, and gain an idea of the extent to which man is a 'portion' of time, not only of space. He is only a portion, or section, of space in regard to his physical, bodily nature. For spiritual perception the past is continually present; the present moment is, at the same time, a real eternity.

What I am explaining to you was once the content of instinctive forms of consciousness. If we really understand ancient records we find a consciousness of this fourfold composition of man and his connection with the cosmos. But this knowledge has been lost to man for many centuries; otherwise he could not have developed the intellect he has today. But we have now reached the point in human evolution when we must again advance from the physical to the really spiritual.

Lecture 6

RESPIRATION, WARMTH AND
THE EGO

3rd February, 1924

WHEN we study human life on earth, we see it proceed in a kind of rhythm expressed in the alternating states of waking and sleeping. It is from this point of view that one must consider what was said in the last lectures about the constitution of man. Let us look, with ordinary consciousness, and in what might be called a purely external way, at the facts before us. In the waking man there is, first, the inner course of his vital processes; but these remain subconscious or unconscious. There is also what we know as sense impressions—that relation to our earthly and cosmic environments which is mediated by the senses. Further, there is the expression of the will—the ability to move as an expression of impulses of will.

Now, when we study man with ordinary cognition we find that the inner life-process, which runs its course in the subconsciousness, continues during sleep; sense activity and the thinking based upon it are, however, suppressed. The expression of the will is also suppressed; likewise the active life of feeling that connects willing and thinking, standing between them to a certain extent.

Now if we simply study, in an unbiased way and without succumbing to preconceived opinions, what we have just found by ordinary consciousness, we are led to say: The processes described as psychical, and the processes taking place between the psychical and the external world, cease in sleep. At most we can say that the dream life finds expression when man sleeps. But we must certainly not assume that these psychical processes are created anew—out of nothing, as it were—every time we wake. This would doubtless be a quite absurd thought, even for ordinary

83

consciousness. On unbiased consideration we must assume that the vehicle of man's psychical processes is also present in sleep. We must admit, however, that this vehicle does not act on man during sleep, i.e. that which evokes in man's senses a consciousness of the external world, and stimulates this consciousness to think, does not act on man in sleep. Moreover, that which sets the body in motion from out of the will is also absent; likewise, what evokes feeling from the organic processes, is not there.

During waking life we are aware that our thoughts act upon our bodily organism. But, with ordinary consciousness, we cannot see how a thought or idea streams down, as it were, into the muscular and bony systems so that the will is involved. Nevertheless, we are aware of this action of our psychic impulses upon our body, and have to recognise that it ceases while we sleep.

Thus even external considerations show us that sleep takes something from man. The only question is, what? If, to begin with, we look at what we have designated man's physical body, we see that it is continually active, in sleep as in the waking state. Moreover, all the processes we described as belonging to the etheric organism continue during sleep. In sleep man grows, he carries on the inner activities of digestion and metabolism, he continues to breathe, etc. All these activities cannot belong to the physical body as such, for they cease when it becomes a corpse. It is then taken over by external, earthly Nature and destroyed. But these destructive forces do not overpower man in sleep; therefore there are counter-forces present, opposing the disintegration of his physical body. Thus we may conclude, from mere external considerations, that the etheric organism is also present during sleep.

Now we know from the preceding lectures that this etheric organism can become an object of knowledge through 'imagination'; one can experience it 'in a picture', just as one experiences the physical body through sense impressions. And we know too that what may be called the astral organism is experienced through 'inspiration'.

We will now go further.—Of course, we could go on drawing conclusions in the above way. But, in the case of the astral body

84

and ego-organisation, we prefer first to study how they actually appear to higher consciousness.

Let us recall how we had to describe the activity of the astral body in man. We saw that it works through the medium of what is airy, or gaseous, in the human organism. Thus we must recognise, to begin with, the astral body in all the activities of the airy element in man.

Now we know that the first and most essential activity of the astral body within the airy element is breathing; and we know from ordinary experience that we have to distinguish between breathing in and breathing out. Further, we know that it is the act of breathing in that vitalises us. We deprive the outer air of its life-giving power and return, not a vitalising, but a devitalising element. Physically speaking, we take in oxygen and give off carbonic acid. But we are not so much concerned with this aspect at the moment; it is the fact of ordinary experience that interests us here: we breathe in the vitalising and breathe out the devitalising element.

The higher knowledge which, as discussed in these last few days, is acquired through 'imagination', 'inspiration', and 'intuition', must now be directed to the life of sleep. We must actually investigate whether there is something that confirms the conclusion to which we were led, namely: that something is lifted out of man when he sleeps.

This question can only be answered by putting and answering another. If there is something that is outside man in sleep, how does it behave when outside?

Well, suppose a man, by such soul exercises as I have described, has actually acquired 'inspiration', i.e. a content for his emptied consciousness. He is now able to receive 'inspired' knowledge. At this stage he can induce the state of sleep artificially; this, however, is no mere sleep but a conscious condition in which the spiritual world flows into him.

I should now like to describe this in quite a crude way. Suppose such a man is able to feel, as it were, in an element of spiritual music, the spiritual beings of the cosmos speaking 'into' him. He will then have certain experiences. But he will also say to himself: These experiences which I now have, reveal something very

85

peculiar; through them what I had to assume as outside of man during sleep no longer remains unknown. What now happens can really be made clear by the following comparison.

Suppose you had a certain experience ten years ago. You have forgotten it, but through something or other you are led to remember it. It has been outside your consciousness; but now, after applying some aid to memory or the like, you recall it. It is now in your consciousness. You have brought back into your consciousness something that was outside it, though connected with you in some way. It is like that with one who has a more inner consciousness and reaches inspiration. The events of sleep begin to emerge, as memories do in ordinary life. Only, the experiences we recall in memory were once in consciousness; the experiences of sleep, however, were not there before. But they enter consciousness in such a way that we really feel we are remembering something not experienced quite consciously before, at least in this life. They come to us like memories. And, as we formerly learnt to understand and experience through memory, we now begin to understand what happens during sleep. Thus into 'inspired' consciousness there simply emerges the experience of what leaves man and remains outside him during sleep, and what was unknown becomes known. We learn to know what it is really doing while he sleeps.

If you were to put into words what you experience with your breath during life, you would say: That I am inwardly permeated with life is owing to the element I breathe in. I cannot owe it to the element I breathe out, for that has the forces of death.

But when, as we saw just now, you are outside your body during sleep, you become extremely partial to the air you breathe out. When awake you did not notice what can be experienced with this exhaled air; you have only heeded the inhaled air which is the vitalising element while you and your soul are within the physical body. But now you have the same—indeed a more exalted—feeling towards the air you so anxiously avoid when you find it accumulated in a room. You express your dislike of the exhaled air. Now the physical body cannot bear it, even in sleep, but your soul and spirit, outside the body, actually breathe in—to put it physically—the carbonic acid you have exhaled.

86

Of course, it is a spiritual, not a physical process; you receive the *impression* made by your exhaled air. In this exhaled air you remain connected with your physical body. You belong to your body, for you say to yourself: There is my body and it is breathing out this devitalising air. You say this unconsciously. You feel yourself connected with your body through its returning the air in this condition. You feel yourself entirely within the air you have exhaled. And this air you breathe out brings you continually the secrets of your inner life. You perceive these, although this perception is, of course, unconscious for the untrained sleeping consciousness. This exhaled air 'sparkles forth' from you and its appearance leads you to say: That is I myself, my inner human being, sparkling out into the universe.

And your own spirit, streaming towards you in the exhaled air has a sun-like appearance.

You now know that man's astral body, when within the physical, delights in the inhaled air, using it unconsciously to set the organic processes in action and induce in them inner mobility. But you also realise that the astral body is outside the physical when you sleep and receives, in its feelings, the secrets of your own human being from the exhaled air. While you ray forth towards the cosmos, your soul beholds unconsciously the inner process involved. Only in 'inspiration' does this become conscious.

Further, we receive a striking impression. It is as if what confronts the sleeping man stood out against a dark background. There is darkness behind, and against this darkness the exhaled air appears luminous: one can put this in no other way. We recognise its essential nature, inasmuch as our everyday thoughts now leave us and the active, cosmic thoughts—the objective, creative thoughts of the world—appear before us in what is flowing out of ourselves. There is the dark background, and the sparkling radiating light; in the latter the creative thoughts gradually arise. The darkness is a veil covering our ordinary, every day thoughts—brain thoughts, as we might call them. We receive a very clear impression that what we regard as most important for physical, earthly life, is darkened as soon as we leave the physical body. And we realise, much more strongly than we could have believed in ordinary consciousness, the dependence of these thoughts upon their physical instrument—the brain. The brain retains these, by an adhesive force as it were. Out there we need no longer 'think' in the sense of everyday life. We behold thoughts; they surge through what appears to us as ourself in the exhaled air.

Thus 'inspired' knowledge perceives how the astral body is in the physical during waking life, initiating, with the help of the inhaled air, the functions it has to perform; how it is outside during sleep and receives the impressions of our own human being. While we are awake the world on which we stand, the world which surrounds us as our earthly environment and the vault of heaven above, form our outer world. When we sleep what is inside our skin, and is otherwise our inner world, becomes our outer world. Only, to begin with, we feel what is here streaming towards us in the exhaled air; it is a *felt* outer world, that we have at first.

And then something further is experienced. The circulation of the blood, which follows closely the process of respiration and remains unconscious during waking life, begins to be very conscious in sleep. It comes before us like a new world, a world, indeed, that we do not merely feel but begin to understand from another point of view than that from which we understand external things with ordinary consciousness. With 'inspired' consciousness—though the will as a life process is present in the unconsciousness of every sleeper—we perceive the circulatory process, just as we perceive external processes of Nature during earthly life. We now come to see that all we do through that will of which we are ordinarily unconscious, involves a counter-process within us.

With every step you transport your body to another place, but something else occurs as well: a warmth-process takes place within you, setting the airy element in motion. This process is the furthest extension of those general processes of metabolism that, like it, occur inwardly and are connected with the circulation of the blood. With ordinary consciousness you observe externally a man's change of place as an expression of his will; but now you look back upon yourself and only find processes occurring within you, and these make up your world.

Truly, what we here behold is not what the theories of present-day science or medicine describe on anatomical grounds. It is a grand spiritual process, a process that conceals innumerable secrets and shows of itself that the real driving power at work within man is not his present ego at all. What man calls his ego in ordinary life is, of course, a mere thought. But it is the ego of man's past lives on earth that is active in him here. In the whole course of these processes, especially of the warmth-processes, you perceive the real ego, working from times long past. Between death and a new birth this ego has undergone an evolution in time; it now works in an entirely spiritual way. You perceive all these metabolic processes, the weakest as well as the most powerful, as the expression of just the highest entity in man.

Moreover, you now perceive that the ego has changed its field of action. It was active within, working upon the breath provided by the mere respiratory process; but now you perceive, from without, the further stages of the warmth-processes that the ego has elaborated from the respiratory processes. You behold the real, active ego of man, working from primeval times and organising him.

You now begin to know that the ego and astral body have actually left the physical and etheric bodies during sleep. They are outside, and now do and experience from without what they otherwise do and experience from within. In ordinary consciousness the ego and astral organisations are still too weak, too little evolved, to experience this consciously. 'Inspiration' really only consists in inwardly organising them so that they are able to perceive what is otherwise imperceptible.

Thus we must actually say: Through 'inspiration' we come to know the astral body of man, through 'intuition', the ego. During sleep, intuition and inspiration are suppressed in the ego and astral body; when they are awakened, man, through them, beholds himself from without. Let us see what this really means.

You remember what I have already said. I spoke of man in his present incarnation (sketch, right centre), and of the etheric body which extends back to a little before birth or conception (yellow); of his astral body which takes him back to the whole period between his last death and his present birth (red); and of

89

'intuition' that takes him back to his previous life on earth (yellow).

Now, to sleep means nothing else than to lead back your consciousness, which is otherwise in the physical body, and to accompany it yourself. Sleep is really a return in time to what I described as past for ordinary consciousness, though nevertheless there. You see, if one really wants to understand the Spiritual,

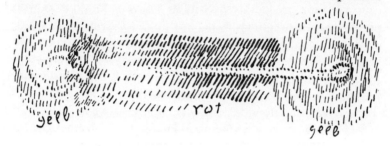

(*gelb*—yellow; *rot*—red)

one must acquire different concepts from those one is accustomed to apply in ordinary life. One must actually realise that every sleep is a return to the regions traversed before birth—or, indeed, to former incarnations. During sleep one actually experiences, though without grasping it, what belongs to one's pre-earthly state and earlier incarnations.

Our concept of time must undergo a complete change. If we ask where a man is when asleep, the reply must be: he is actually in his pre-earthly state, or has returned to his former lives on earth. When talking simply we say: he is 'outside' his body. The reality is as I have explained. It is this that manifests as the rhythmic alternation of waking and sleeping.

All this becomes quite different at death. The most striking change is, of course, that man leaves his physical body behind in the earthly realm, where it is received, disintegrated and destroyed by the forces of the physical world. It can no longer give rise to the impressions I described as being made upon the sleeping man through the medium of the exhaled air. For the physical body no longer breathes; with all its functions it is now lost to man. There is something, however, that is not lost—and even ordinary consciousness can see that this is so. Thinking, feeling and willing live in our soul, but over and above these we have something very special, namely: memory. We do not only think about what is at present before, or around, us; our inner life contains fragments of what we have experienced, and these re-arise as thoughts. Now those people, often somewhat peculiar, who are known as psychologists have developed quite curious ideas about memory. These investigators of the human soul say something like this: man uses his senses; he perceives this or that and thinks about it. He has then a thought. He goes away and forgets the whole thing. But after a time he recalls it; the memory of what has been, re-appears. Man can recall what is past and has been out of his mind meanwhile; he can bring it to mind again. On this account, these people think that man forms a thought from his experience, this thought descends somewhere, to rest as it were in some chest or box and to re-appear when remembered. Either it bobs up of its own accord, or has to be fetched.

This sort of thing is a very model of confused thinking. For the whole belief that the thought is waiting somewhere whence it can be fetched, does not correspond to the facts at all. Just compare an immediate perception which you have, and to which you link a thought, with the way an image of memory, or a memory-thought, arises. You make no distinction at all. You receive a sense impression from without, and a thought links itself thereto. The thought is there; but what lies behind the sense impression and calls forth the thought, you usually speak of as unknown. The memory-thought that arises from within you is, indeed, no different from the thought that emerges for outer perception. In one case—representing it schematically—you have man's environment (yellow); the thought presents itself from without in connection with this environment (red); in the other it comes from within. The latter is a memory-thought (vertical arrow). The direction from which it comes is different.

While we are perceiving—experiencing—anything, something is continually going on beneath the mental presentation, beneath our thinking. It is really as follows: Thought accompanies perception. Our perceptions enter our body, whereas our thought 'stands out'. Something does enter our body, and this we do not perceive. This goes on while we are thinking about the experience, and an 'impression' is made. It is not thought that passes down but something quite different. It is this something that evokes the process which we perceive later and of which we form the memory-thought—just as we form a thought of the outer world. The thought is always in the present moment. Even unprejudiced observation shows that this is so. The thought is not preserved somewhere or other as in a casket, but a process occurs which

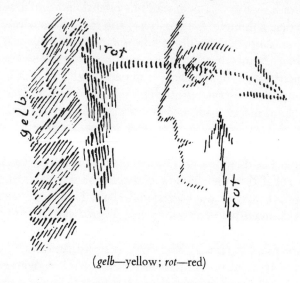

(*gelb*—yellow; *rot*—red)

the act of memory transforms into a thought—just as we transform outer perception into a thought.

I must burden you with these considerations, or you will not really come to an understanding of memory. That the thought does not want to go right down, is known to children—and to grown up people, too, in special cases—though only half consciously. So, when we want to memorise something, we have recourse to extraneous aids. Just think how many people find it helps to repeat a thing aloud; others make curious gestures when they want to fix something in their minds. The point is that an entirely different process runs parallel to the mere process of mental presentation. What we remember is really the smallest part of what is here involved.

Between waking up and falling asleep we move about the

world, receiving impressions from all sides. We only attend to a few, but they all attend to us. It is a rich world that lives in the depths of our being, but only some few fragments are received into our thoughts. This world is like a deep ocean confined within us. The mental presentations of memory surge up like single waves, but the ocean remains within. It has not been given us by the physical world, nor can the physical world take it away. When man sheds his physical body, this whole world is there, bound up with his etheric body. Upon this all his experiences have been impressed, and these man bears within him immediately after death. In a certain sense, they are 'rolled up' in him.

Now man's first experience, immediately after death, is of everything that has made its impression upon him. Not only the ordinary shreds of memory which arise during earthly consciousness, but his whole earthly life, with all that has 'impressed' him stands before him now. But he would have to remain in eternal contemplation of this earthly life of his if something else did not happen to his etheric body, something different from what happens to the physical body through the earth and its forces. The earthly elements take over the physical body and destroy it; the cosmic ether, working (as I told you) from the periphery, streams in and dispels in all directions what has been impressed upon the etheric body. Thus man's next experience is as follows: During earthly life many, many things have made their impression upon me. All this has entered my etheric body. I now survey it, but it becomes more and more indistinct. It is as if I were looking at a tree that had made a strong impression upon me during my life. At first I see it life-size, as when it made its impression upon me from physical space. But it now grows, becomes larger and more shadowy; it becomes larger and larger, gigantic but more and more shadowy. Now it is like that with a human being whom I have learnt to know in his physical form. Immediately after death I have him before me as he impressed himself upon my etheric body. He now increases in size, becomes more and more shadowy. Everything grows, becomes more and more shadowy until it fills the whole universe, becomes thereby quite shadowy, and completely disappears.

This lasts some days. Everything has become gigantic and

shadowy, thereby diminishing in intensity. Man sheds his second corpse; or, strictly speaking, the cosmos takes it from him. He is now in his ego and astral body. What had been impressed upon his etheric body is now within the cosmos; it has flowed out into the cosmos. We see the working of the universe behind the veils of our existence.

We are placed in the world as human beings. In the course of earthly life the whole world works upon us. We roll it all together in a certain sense. The world gives us much and we hold it together. The moment we die the world takes back what it has given. But it is something new that it receives, for we have experienced it all in a particular way. The world receives our whole experience and impresses it upon its own ether.

We now stand in the universe and say to ourselves, as we consider, first of all, this experience with our etheric body: truly, we are not only here for ourselves; the universe has its own intentions in regard to us. It has put us here that its own content may pass through us and be received again in the form into which we can transmute it. As human beings we are not here for our own ends alone; in respect to our etheric body, for example, we are here for the universe. The universe needs us because, through us, it 'fulfils' itself—fills itself again and again with its own content. There is an interchange, not of substance but of thoughts between the universe and man. The universe gives its cosmic thoughts to our etheric body and receives them back again in a humanised condition. We are not here for ourselves alone; we are here for the sake of the universe.

Now a thought like this should not remain merely theoretical and abstract; indeed it cannot. If it were to remain a mere thought, we would have to be creatures of pasteboard, not men with living feelings. In saying this I do not deny that our civilisation really does tend to make people often as apathetic towards such things as if they really were made of pasteboard. Civilised people today often appear to be such pasteboard figures. A thought like this preserves our human feeling and sympathy with the world, and leads us directly to the point from which we started. We began by saying that man feels himself estranged from the world in a two-fold way: on the one hand, in regard to external Nature which, he must admit, only destroys him as physical body; on the other hand, in regard to his inner life of soul which, again and again, lights up and dies away. This becomes for him a riddle of the universe. But now, as a result of spiritual study, man begins to feel himself no mere stranger in the universe. The universe has something to give him, and takes from him something in turn. Man begins to feel his inner kinship with the world. He now sees in a new light the two thoughts that I have put before you and which are really cosmic thoughts, namely:

Thou, O Nature, canst only destroy my physical body.

I, myself, have no kinship with thee, in spite of the thinking, feeling and willing of my inner life. Thou lightest up and diest down; and in my inner being I have no kinship with thee.

These two thoughts, evoked in us by the riddles of the universe, now appear in a new light, for we begin to feel ourselves akin to the cosmos and an organic part of its whole life. Thus anthroposophical reflection begins by making friends with the world, really learning to know the world that, on external observation, repulsed us at first. Anthroposophical knowledge makes us be-become more human. If we cannot bring to it this quality of heart, this mood of feeling, we are not taking it in the right way. One might compare theoretical anthroposophy to a photograph. If you are very anxious to learn to know someone you have once met, or with whom you have been brought into touch through something or other, you would not want to be offered a photograph. You may find pleasure in the photograph; but it cannot kindle the warmth of your feeling life, for the man's living presence does not confront you.

Theoretical Anthroposophy is a photograph of what Anthroposophy intends to be. It intends to be a living presence; it really wants to use words, concepts and ideas in order that something living may shine down from the spiritual world into the physical. Anthroposophy does not only want to impart knowledge; it seeks to awaken life. This it can do; though, of course, to feel life we must bring life to meet it.

Lecture 7

DREAM-LIFE AND EXTERNAL REALITY

8th February, 1924

IN the last lectures I have already drawn your attention to the way the Science of Initiation must speak of the alternating states of sleeping and waking, which are known to us from ordinary consciousness and through which we can really find a path of approach—*one* path of approach—to the secrets of human life. It is a *life* that finds expression while we sleep—soul life, dream life, a life that ordinary consciousness, if free from mystical or similar tendencies, does not take seriously at first. This attitude is certainly justified; the sober-minded man does not take his dream-life seriously and, to a certain extent, he is right, for he sees that it shows him all kinds of pictures and reminiscences of his ordinary life. When he compares his dream-life with his ordinary experience, he must, of course, hold fast to the latter and call it reality. But the dream-life comes with its re-combinations of ordinary experiences; and if man asks himself what it really signifies for the totality of his being, he can find no answer in ordinary consciousness.

Let us now consider this dream-life as it presents itself to us. We can distinguish two different kinds of dreams. The first conjures pictures of outer experiences before our soul. Years ago, or a few days maybe, we experienced this or that in a definite way; now a dream conjures up a picture more or less similar—usually dissimilar—to the external experience. If we discover the connection between this dream-picture and the external experience, we are at once struck by the transformation the latter has undergone. We do not usually relate the dream-picture to a particular experience in the outer world, for the resemblance does not strike us. Nevertheless, if we look more closely at this type of dream-life that conjures outer experiences in transformed pictures before the soul, we find that something in us takes' hold of these experiences; we cannot, however, retain them as we can in the waking state, when we have full use of our bodily organs and experience the images of memory which resemble external life as far as possible. In memory we have pictures of outer life that are more or less true. Of course there are people who dream in their memories, but this is regarded as abnormal. In our memories we have, more or less, true pictures, in our dreams, transformed pictures of outer life. That is one kind of dream.

There is, however, another kind, and this is really much more important for a knowledge of the dream-life. It is the kind in which, for example, a man dreams of seeing a row of white pillars, one of which is damaged or dirty; he wakes up with this dream and finds he has toothache. He then sees that the row of pillars 'symbolises' the row of teeth; one tooth is aching, and this is represented by the damaged or, perhaps, dirty pillar. Or a man may wake up dreaming of a seething stove and find he has palpitation of the heart. Or he is distressed in his dream by a frog approaching his hand; he takes hold of the frog and finds it soft. He shudders, and wakes up to find he is holding a corner of his blanket, grasped in sleep. These things can go much further. A man may dream of all kinds of snake-like forms and wake up with intestinal pains.

So we see that there is a second kind of dream which gives pictorial, symbolic expression to man's inner organs. When we have grasped this, we learn to interpret many dream-figures in just this way. For example, we may dream of entering a vaulted cellar. The ceiling is black and covered with cobwebs; a repulsive sight. We wake up to find we have a headache. The interior of the skull is expressed in the vaulted cellar; we even notice that the cerebral convolutions are symbolised in the peculiar formations constituting the vault. If we pursue our studies further in this direction we find that all our organs can appear in dreams in this pictorial way.

Here, indeed, is something that points very clearly, by means of the dream, to the whole inner life of man. There are people who, while actually asleep and dreaming, compose subjects for quite good paintings. If you have studied these things you will know what particular organ is depicted, though in an altered, symbolic form. Such paintings sometimes possess unusual beauty; and when the artist is told what organ he has really symbolised so beautifully, he is quite startled, for he has not the same respect for his organs that he has for his paintings.

These two kinds of dream can be easily distinguished by one who is prepared to study the world of dreams in an intimate way. In one kind of dream we have pictures of experiences undergone in the outer world; in the other, pictorial representations of our own internal organs.

Now it is comparatively easy to pursue the study of dreams as far as this. Most people whose attention has been called to the existence of these two kinds will recall experiences of their own that justify this classification.

But to what does this classification point? Well, if you examine the first kind of dreams, studying the special kind of pictures contained, you find that widely different external experiences can be represented by the same dream; again, one and the same experience can be depicted in different people by different dreams.

Take the case of a man who dreams he is approaching a mountain. There is a cave-like opening and into this the sun is still shining. He dreams he goes in. It soon begins to grow dark, then quite dark. He gropes his way forward, encounters an obstacle, and feels there is a little lake before him. He is in great danger, and the dream takes a dramatic course.

Now a dream like this can represent very different external experiences. The picture I have just described may relate to a railway accident in which the dreamer was once involved. What he experienced at that time finds expression now, perhaps years afterwards, in the dream described. The pictures are quite different from what he had experienced. He could have been in a shipwreck, or a friend may have proved unfaithful, and so on. If you compare the dream-picture with the actual experience, studying them in this intimate way, you will find that the content of the pictures is not really of great importance; it is the dramatic sequence that is significant: whether a feeling of expectation was present, whether this is relieved, or leads to a crisis. One might say that the whole complex of feelings is translated into the dream-life.

Now, if we start from here and examine dreams of this (first) type, we find that the pictures derive their whole character chiefly from the nature of the man himself, from the individuality of his ego. (Only, we must not study dreams like the psychiatrists who bring everything under one hat.) If we have an understanding of dreams—I say, of dreams, not of dream-interpretation—we can often learn to know a man better from his dreams than from observing his external life. When we study all that a person experiences in such dreams we find that it always points back to the experience of the ego in the outer world.

On the other hand, when we study the second kind of dream, we find that what it conjures before the soul in dream pictures is *only* experienced in a dream. For, when awake, man experiences the form of his organs at most by studying scientific anatomy and physiology. That, however, is not a real *experience*; it is merely looking at them externally, as one looks at stones and plants. So we may ignore it and say that, in the ordinary consciousness of daily life, man experiences very little, or nothing at all, of his internal organism. The second kind of dream, however, puts this before him in pictures, although in transformed pictures.

Now, if we study a man's life, we find that it is governed by his ego—more or less, according to his strength of will and character. But the activity of the ego within human life very strongly resembles the first kind of dream-experience. Just try to examine closely whether a person's dreams are such that in them his experiences are greatly, violently altered. In anyone who has such dreams you will find a man of strong will-nature. On the other hand, a man who dreams his life almost as it actually is, not altering it in his dreams, will be found to be a man of weak will.

Thus you see the action of the ego within a man's life expressed in the way he shapes his dreams. Such knowledge shows us that we have to relate dreams of the first kind to the human ego. Now we learnt in the last lectures that the ego and astral body are outside the physical and etheric bodies in sleep. Remembering this, we shall not be surprised to learn that Spiritual Science shows

99

us that the ego then takes hold of the pictures of waking life—those pictures that it otherwise takes hold of in ordinary reality through the physical and etheric bodies. The first kind of dream is an activity of the ego outside the physical and etheric bodies.

What, then, is the second kind of dream? Of course it, too, must have something to do with what is outside the physical and etheric bodies during sleep. It cannot be the ego, for this knows nothing of the symbolic organ-forms presented by the dream. One is forced to see that it is the astral body of man that, in sleep, shapes these symbolic pictures of the inner organs, as the ego the pictures of external experience. Thus the two kinds of dreams point to the activity of the ego and astral body between falling asleep and waking up.

We can go further. We have seen what a weak and what a strong man does in his dreams; we have seen that the weak man dreams of things almost exactly as he experienced them, while the strong man transforms and re-arranges them, colouring them by his own character. Pursuing this to the end, we can compare our result with a man's behaviour in waking life. We then discover the following intensely interesting fact. Let a man tell you his dreams; notice how one dream-picture is linked to another; study the configuration of his dreams. Then, having formed an idea of the way he dreams, look at the man himself. Stimulated by the idea you have formed of his dream-life, you will be able to form a good picture of the way he acts in life. This leads us to remarkable secrets of human nature. If you study a man as he acts in life and learn to know his individual character, you will find that only a part of his actions proceeds from his own being, from his ego. If all depended on the ego, a man would really do what he dreams; the violent character would be as violent in life as in his dreams, while one who leaves his life almost unchanged in his dreams, would hold aloof from life at all points, let it take its course, let things happen, shaping his life as little as he shapes his dreams.

And what a man does over and above this—how does that happen? My dear friends, we can very well say that it is done by God, by the spiritual beings of the world. All that man does, he does not do himself. In fact, he does just as much as he actually dreams; the rest is done through him and to him. Only, in ordinary life we do not train ourselves to observe these things; otherwise we would discover that we only actively participate in the deeds of life as much as we actively participate in our dreams. The world hinders the violent man from being as violent in life as in dreams; in the weak man instincts are working, and once more life itself adds that which happens through him, and of which he would not dream.

It is interesting to observe a man in some action of his life and to ask: what comes from him, and what from the world? From him proceeds just as much as he can dream, no more, no less. The world adds something in the case of a weak man, and subtracts something in the case of a violent man. Seen in this light, dreams become extraordinarily interesting and give us deep insight into the being of man.

Many of the things I have been saying have, it is true, dawned upon psycho-analysts in a distorted, caricatured form. But they are not able to look into what lives and weaves in human nature, so distort it all. From what I have put before you today in a quite external way, you can see the necessity of acquiring a subtle, delicate knowledge of the soul if one wants to handle such things at all; otherwise one can know nothing of the relations between dreams and external reality as realised by man in his life. Hence I once described psycho-analysis as dilettantism, because it knows nothing of man's outer life. But it also knows nothing of man's inner life. These two dilettantisms do not merely add, they must be multiplied; for ignorance of the inner life mars the outer, and ignorance of the outer life mars the inner. Multiplying d × d we get d-squared: $d \times d = d^2$. Psycho-analysis is dilettantism raised to the second power.

If we study the alternating states of waking and sleeping in this intimate way, we can perceive and understand so much of the essential nature of man that we are really led to the portal of the Science of Initiation.

Now consider something else that I told you in these lectures: the fact that man can strengthen his soul forces by exercises, by meditations; that he then advances beyond the ordinary more or less empty, abstract thinking to a thinking inherently pictorial, called 'imagination'. Now it was necessary to explain that man, progressing in 'imagination', comes to apprehend his whole life as an etheric impulse entering earthly life through conception and birth—strictly speaking, from before conception and birth. Through dreams he receives reminiscences of what he has experienced externally since descending to earth for his present life. 'Imagination' gives us pictures which, in the way they are experienced, can be very like dream-pictures; but they contain, not reminiscences of this earthly life, but of what preceded it. It is quite ridiculous for people who do not know Spiritual Science to say that imaginations may be dreams too. They ought only to consider what it is that we 'dream of' in imaginations. We do not dream of what the senses offer; the content represents man's being before he was endowed with senses. Imagination leads man to a new world.

Nevertheless there is a strong resemblance between the *second* kind of dream and imaginative experience when first acquired through soul exercises. We experience pictures, mighty pictures—and this in all clarity, we might say exactness. We experience a universe of pictures, so wonderful, so rich in colour, so majestic that we have nothing else in our consciousness. If we would paint these pictures, we should have to paint a mighty tableau; but we could only capture the appearance of a single moment—just as we cannot paint a flash of lightning, but only its momentary appearance, for all this takes its course in time. Still, if we only arrest a single moment we obtain a mighty picture.

Let us represent this diagrammatically. Naturally, this will not be very like what we behold; nevertheless, this sketch will illustrate what I mean.

Look at this sketch I have drawn. It has an inner configuration and includes the most varied forms. It is inwardly and outwardly immense. If, now, we become stronger and stronger in concentrating, in holding fast the picture, it does not merely come before us for one moment. We must seize it with presence of mind; otherwise it eludes us before we can bring it into the present moment. Altogether, presence of mind is required in spiritual observation. If we are not only able to apply sufficient presence of mind in order to seize and become conscious of it at all, but can retain it, it contracts and, instead of being something all-embracing, becomes smaller and smaller, moving onward in time. It

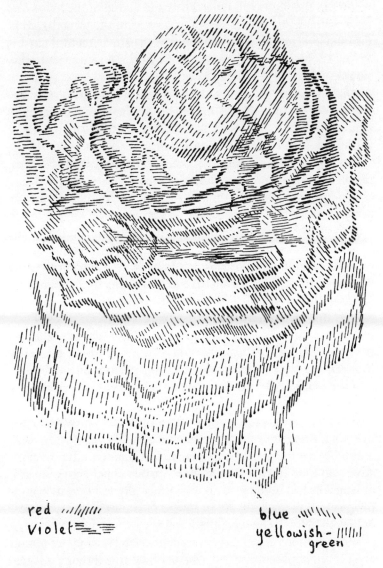

red ,,,/,//////
violet ⹀⹀⹀

blue ,ıı'\\,,,
yellowish- //////
green

suddenly shrinks into something; one part becomes the human head, another the human lung, a third the human liver. The physical matter provided by the mother's body only fills out what enters from the spiritual world and becomes man. At length we say: what the liver is we now see spiritually in a mighty picture in the pre-earthly life. The same is true of the lung. And now we may compare it with the content of the second kind of dream. Here, too, an organ may appear to us in a beautiful picture, as I said before, but this is very poor compared to what imagination reveals.

Thus we gain the impression that imagination gives us something created by a great master-hand, the dream something clumsy. But they both point in the same direction and represent, spiritually, man's internal organisation.

It is but a step from this to another and very true idea. When, through imagination, we discern the pre-earthly human being as a mighty etheric picture, and see this mighty etheric picture crystallise—as it were—into the physical man, we are led to ask what would happen if the dream-pictures, those relating to the inner organs, began to develop the same activity. We find that a caricature of the inner organs would arise. The human liver, so perfect in its way, is formed from an imaginative picture that points to the pre-earthly life. If the dream-picture were to become a liver, this would not be a human liver, not even a goose-liver, but a caricature of a liver. This gives us, in fact, deep insight into the whole being of man. For there is really some similarity between the dream-picture and the imaginative picture, as we now see quite clearly. And we cannot help asking how this comes about.

Well, we can go still further. Take the dream pictures of the first kind, those linked to outer-experiences. To begin with, there is nothing resembling these in imaginative cognition. But imaginative cognition reaches back to a pre-earthly experience of man's, in which he had nothing to do with other physical human beings. Imaginative vision leads to an image of pre-earthly experiences of the spirit. Just think what this implies.

When we look into man's inner life we receive the impression that certain symbolic pictures, whether they arise through imagination or in dreams [of the second kind], refer to what is within man, man's internal organisation; on the other hand, the imaginations which refer to outer experiences are connected, neither with man's internal organisation nor with outer life, but with experiences of his pre-earthly state. Beside these imaginations one can only place dream experiences of the first kind, those relating to external experiences of earthly life; but there is no inner connection here between *these* imaginations and *these* dreams. Such a connection only exists for dreams of the second kind.

Now, what do I intend by all these descriptions? I want to draw your attention to an intimate way of studying human life, a way that propounds real riddles. Man really observes life in a most superficial manner today. If he would study it more exactly, more intimately, he would notice the things I have spoken about in this lecture. In a certain sense, however, he does notice them; only, he does not actually know it. He is not really aware how strongly his dreams influence his life. He regards a dream as a flitting phantom, for he does not know that his ego is active in one kind of dream, his astral body in another. But if we seek to grasp still deeper phenomena of life, the riddles to which I referred become more insistent. Those who have been here some time will have already heard me relate such facts as the following: There is a pathological condition in which a person loses his connection with his life in memory. I have mentioned the case of an acquaintance of mine who one day, without his conscious knowledge, left his home and family, went to the station, bought a ticket and travelled, like a sleep-walker, to another station. Here he changed, bought another ticket and travelled further. He did this for a long time. He commenced his journey at a town in South Germany. It was found later, when the case was investigated, that he had been in Budapest, Lemberg (Poland), etc. At last, as his consciousness began to function again, he found himself in a casual ward in Berlin, where he had finally landed. Some weeks had passed before his arrival at the shelter, and these were quite obliterated from his consciousness. He remembered the last thing he had done at home; the rest was obliterated. It was necessary to trace his journey by external inquiries.

You see, his ego was not present in what he was doing. If you study the literature of this subject you will find hundreds and hundreds of cases of such intermittent ego-consciousness. What have we here? If you took trouble to study the dream-world of such a patient you would discover something peculiar. To begin with, you would find that, at least at certain periods of his life, the patient had had the most vivid dreams imaginable, dreams that were especially characterised by his making up his mind to do something, forming certain intentions.

Now, if you study the dreams of a normal person you will find intentions playing a very small part, if any. People dream all sorts of wonderful things, but intentions play no part, as a rule. When intentions do play a part in a dream, we usually wake up laughing at ourselves for entertaining them. But if you study the dream-life of such people with intermittent consciousness, you will find that they entertain intentions in their dreams and, on waking, take these very seriously; indeed, they take these so seriously that they feel pangs of conscience if unable to carry them out. Often these intentions are so foolish in the face of the external physical world that it is not possible to carry them out; this hurts such people and makes them quite excited. To take dreams seriously—especially in regard to their *intentions* (not *wishes*)—is the counterpart of this condition of obliterated consciousness.

One who is able to observe human beings can tell, in certain circumstances, whether a person is liable to suffer in this way. Such people have something which shows they never quite wake up in regard to certain inner and outer experiences. One gradually finds that such a person goes too far with his ego out of his physical and etheric bodies in sleep; every night he goes too far into the spiritual and cannot carry back into the physical and etheric bodies what he has experienced. At last, because he has so often not brought it completely back, it holds him outside—i.e. what he experiences too deeply within the spiritual holds the ego back and he passes into a condition in which the ego is not in the physical body.

In such a radical case as this it is especially interesting to observe the dream-life. This differs from the dream-life of our ordinary contemporaries; it is much more interesting, but of course this has its reverse side. Still, objectively considered, illness is more interesting than health; from the subjective side—i.e. for the person concerned, as well as from the point of view of ordinary life, it is another matter. For a knowledge of the human being the dream-life of such a patient is really much more interesting than the dream-life of an ordinary contemporary.

In such a case you actually see a kind of connection between the ego and the whole dream-world; one might say, it is almost tangible. And we are led to ask the following questions: What is the relation of the dream pictures that refer to internal organs, to the imaginations that also refer to internal organs?

Well, viewed 'externally', the pictures of man's inner organisation that are given in imagination, point to what was within man before he had his earthly body, before he was on the earth; the dream-pictures arise when once he is here. The imaginations point to the past, the dream-pictures to the present. But though an ordinary dream-picture that refers to an internal organ would correspond to a caricature of that organ, while the imagination would correspond to the perfect organ, nevertheless the caricature has the inherent possibility of growing into a perfect organ.

This leads us to the studies we shall be pursuing tomorrow. They centre in the question: Does the content of such an imagination relate to man's past life, and is the dream the beginning of the imagination of the future? Will a dream-picture of today evolve into the imagination to which we shall be able to look back in a future life on earth? Is the content of the dream perhaps the seed of the content of the imagination?

This significant question presents itself to us. What we have gained through a study of dreams is here seen in conjunction with the question of man's repeated lives on earth. You see, moreover, that we must really look more deeply into the life of man than we usually find convenient; otherwise we shall find no point of contact with what the Science of Initiation says about the being of man.

By such a lecture as this I wanted especially to awaken in you some idea of the superficial way man is studied in the civilisation of today, and of the need of intimate observation in all directions. Such intimate observation leads at once to Spiritual Science.

Lecture 8

DREAMS, IMAGINATIVE COGNITION, AND THE BUILDING OF DESTINY

9th February, 1924

YESTERDAY I tried to show how a more intimate study of man's dream-life can lead us towards the Science of Initiation. To a certain extent, the point of view was that of ordinary consciousness. Today it will be my task to enter more deeply into the same subject-matter from the point of view of 'imaginative' cognition—i.e. to present what we were studying yesterday as it appears to one who has learnt to see the world in 'imaginations'.

For the moment we will neglect the difference between the two kinds of dreams discussed yesterday, and consider dreams as such. It will be a sound approach to describe 'imaginative' vision in relation to dreams which a man endowed with imagination may have. Let us compare such a dream with the self-perception attained by the imaginative seer when he looks back upon his own being—when he observes imaginatively his own or another's organs—or, perhaps, the whole human being as a complete organism. You see, the appearance of the dream-world to imaginative consciousness is quite different from its appearance to ordinary consciousness. The same is true of the physical and etheric organism. Now the imaginative seer can dream too; and under certain circumstances his dreams will be just as chaotic as those of other people. From his own experience he can quite well judge the world of dreams; for, side by side with the imaginative life that is inwardly co-ordinated, clear and luminous, the dream-world runs its ordinary course, just as it does side by side with waking life. I have often emphasised that one who attains really spiritual perception does not become a dreamer or enthusiast, living only in the higher worlds and not seeing external reality. People who are ever dreaming in higher worlds, or about them, and do not see external reality, are not initiates; they should be considered from a pathological point of view, at least in the psychological sense of the term. The real knowledge of initiation does not estrange one from ordinary, physical life and its various relationships. On the contrary, it makes one a more painstaking, conscientious observer than without the faculty of seership. Indeed we may say: if a man has no sense of ordinary realities, no interest in ordinary realities, no interest in the details of others' lives, if he is so 'superior' that he sails through life without troubling about its details, he shows he is not a genuine seer. A man with imaginative cognition—he may, of course, also have 'inspired' and 'intuitive' cognition, but at present I am only speaking of 'imagination'—is quite well acquainted with dream-life from his own experience. Nevertheless, his conception of dreams is different. He feels the dream as something with which he is connected, with which he unites himself much more strongly than is possible through ordinary consciousness. He can take dreams more seriously. Indeed, only imagination justifies us taking our dreams seriously, for it enables us to look, as it were, behind dreaming and apprehend its dramatic course—its tensions, resolutions, catastrophes, and crises—rather than its detailed content. The individual content interests us less, even before we acquire imagination; we are more interested in studying whether the dream leads to a crisis, or to inner joy, to something that we find easy or that proves difficult—and the like.

It is the course of the dream—just that which does not interest ordinary consciousness and which I can only call the dramatic quality of the dream—that begins to interest us most. We see behind the scenes of dream-life and, in doing so, become aware that we have before us something related to man's spiritual being in quite a definite way. We see that, in a spiritual sense, the dream *is* the human being, as the seed is the plant. And in this 'seed-like' man we learn to grasp what is really foreign to his present life— just as the seed taken from the plant in the autumn of a given year is foreign to the plant's life of that year and will only be at home in the plant-growth of the following year.

It is just this way of studying the dream that gives imaginative consciousness its strongest impressions; for, in our own dreaming being, we detect more and more that we bear within us something that passes over to our next life on earth, germinating between death and a new birth and growing on into our next earthly life. It is the seed of this next earthly life that we learn to feel in the dream.

This is extremely important and is further confirmed by comparing this special experience, which is an intense experience of feeling, with the perception we can have of a physical human being standing before us with his several organs. This perception, too, changes for imaginative consciousness, so that we feel like we do when a fresh, green, blossoming plant we have known begins to fade. When, in imaginative consciousness, we observe the lungs, liver, stomach, and, most of all, the brain as physical organs, we say to ourselves that these, in respect to the physical, are all withering.

Now you will say that it cannot be pleasant to confront, in imaginations, a physical man as a withering being. Well, no one who knows the Science of Initiation will tell you it is only there to offer pleasant truths to men. It has to tell the truth, not please. On the other hand, it must be remembered that, while we learn to know the physical man as a withering being, we perceive in him the spiritual man; in a sense, you cannot see the spiritual man shine forth without learning to know the physical as a decaying, withering being.

Thus man's appearance does not thereby become uglier but more beautiful—and truer, too. And when one is able to perceive the withering of man's organs, which is such a spiritual process, these organs with their etheric content appear as something that has come over from the past—from the last life on earth—and is now withering. In this way we really come to see that the seed of a future life is being formed within the withering process that proceeds from man's *being* of a former life on earth.

The human head is withering most; and the dream appears to imaginative perception as an emanation of the human head. On the other hand, the metabolic and limb organism appears to imaginative vision to be withering least of all. It appears very similar to the ordinary dream; it is least faded and most closely united, in form and content, with the future of man. The rhythmic organisation contained in the chest is the connecting link between them, holding the balance. It is just to spiritual perception that the human heart appears as a remarkable organ. It, too, is seen to be withering; nevertheless, seen imaginatively, it retains almost its physical form, only beautified and ennobled (I say 'almost', not 'completely').

There would be a certain amount of truth in painting man's spiritual appearance as follows: a countenance comparatively wise looking, perhaps even somewhat aged; hands and feet small and childlike; wings to indicate remoteness from the earth; and the heart indicated in some form or other reminiscent of the physical organ.

If we can perceive the human being imaginatively, such a picture which we might attempt to paint will not be symbolic in the bad sense that symbolism has today. It will not be empty and insipid, but will contain elements of physical existence while, at the same time, transcending the physical. One might also say, speaking paradoxically (one must begin to speak in paradoxes to some extent when one speaks of the spiritual world, for the spiritual world does really appear quite different from the physical): When we begin to perceive man with imagination we feel in regard to his head: How intensely I must think, if I am to hold my own against this head! Contemplating the human head with imaginative consciousness one gradually comes to feel quite feeble-minded, for with the acutest thoughts acquired in daily life one cannot easily approach this wonderful physical structure of the human head. It is now transformed into something spiritual and its form is still more wonderful as it withers, showing its form so clearly. For the convolutions of the brain actually seem to contain, in a withered form, deep secrets of the world's structure. When we begin to understand the human head we gaze deeply into these cosmic secrets, yet feel ourselves continually baffled in our attempts.

On the other hand, when we try to understand the metabolic and limb system with imaginative consciousness, we say to ourselves: Your keen intellect does not help you here; you ought

properly to sleep and dream of man, for man only appre-
hends this part of his organisation by dreaming of it while
awake.

So you see, we must proceed to a highly differentiated mode
of perception when we begin to study man's physical organisation
imaginatively. We must become clever, terribly clever, when we
study his head. We must become dreamers when studying his
system of limbs and metabolism. And we must really swing to
and fro, as it were, between dreaming and waking if we want to
grasp, in imaginative vision, the wonderful structure of man's
rhythmic system. But all this appears as the relic of his last life on
earth. What he experiences in the waking state is the relic of his
last life; this plays into his present life, giving him as much as I
ascribed to him yesterday when I said of his life of action, for
example, that only as much of man's actions as he can dream of is
really done by himself; the rest is done by the gods in and through
him. The present is active to this extent; all the rest comes from
his former earthly lives. We see that this is so when we have a
man before us and perceive his withering physical organisation.
And if we look at what man knows of himself while he dreams—
dreams in his *sleep*—we have before us what man is preparing for
the next life on earth. These things can be easily distinguished.

Thus imagination leads directly from a study of the waking
and sleeping man to a perception of his development from earthly
life to earthly life.

Now what is preserved in memory occupies a quite special place
in the waking and in the sleeping man. Consider your ordinary
memories. What you remember you draw forth from within
you in the form of thoughts or mental presentations; you represent to yourself past experiences. These, as you know, lose in
memory their vividness, impressiveness, colour, etc. Remembered experiences are pale. But, on the other hand, memory
cannot but appear to be very closely connected with man's being;
indeed it appears to be his very being. Man is not usually honest
enough in his soul to make the necessary confession to himself;
but I ask you to look into yourself to find out what you really are
in respect to what you call your ego. Is there anything there beside
your memories? If you try to get to your ego you will scarcely

find anything else but your life's memories. True, you find these permeated by a kind of activity, but this remains very shadowy and dim. It is your memories that, for earthly life, appear as your living ego.

Now this world of memories which you need only call to mind in order to realise how entirely shadowy they are—what does it become in imaginative cognition? It 'expands' at once; it becomes a mighty tableau through which we survey, in pictures, all that we have experienced in our present life on earth. One might say: If this* be man, and this the memory within him, imagination at once extends this memory back to his birth. One feels oneself outside of space; here all consists of events. One gazes into a tableau and surveys one's whole life up to the present. Time becomes space. It is like looking down an avenue; one takes in one's whole past in a tableau, or panorama, and can speak of memory expanding. In ordinary consciousness memory is confined, as it were, to a single moment at a time. Indeed, it is really as follows: If, for example, we have reached the age of forty and are recalling, not in 'imagination', but in ordinary consciousness, something experienced twenty years ago, it is as if it were far off in space, yet still there. Now—in imaginative cognition—it has remained; it has no more disappeared than the distant trees of an avenue. It is there. This is how we gaze into the tableau and know that the memory we bear with us in ordinary consciousness is a serious illusion. To take it for a reality is like taking a cross-section of a tree trunk for the tree trunk itself. Such a section is really nothing at all; the trunk is above and below the mere picture thus obtained. Now it is really like that when we perceive memories in imaginative cognition. We detect the utter unreality of the individual items; the whole expands almost as far as birth—in certain circumstances even farther. All that is past becomes present; it is there, though at the periphery.

Once we have grasped this, once we have attained this perception, we can know—and re-observe at any moment—that man reviews this tableau when he leaves his physical body at death. This lasts some days and is his natural life-element. On passing through the gate of death man gazes, to begin with, at his life in

* The drawing is not reproduced.

113

mighty, luminous, impressive pictures. This constitutes his experience for some days.

But we must now advance farther in imaginative cognition. As we do so our life is enriched in a certain way and we accordingly understand many things in a different way from before. Consider, for example, our behaviour towards other people. In ordinary life we may, in individual cases, think about the intentions we have had, the actions we have performed—our whole attitude towards others. We think about all this, more or less, according as we are more or less reflective persons. But now all this stands before us. In our idea of our behaviour we only grasp a part of the full reality. Suppose we have done another a service or an injury. We learn to see the results of our good deed, the satisfaction to the other man, perhaps his furtherance in this or that respect—i.e. we see the results which may follow our deed in the physical world. If we have done an evil deed, we come to see we have injured him, we see that he remained unsatisfied or, perhaps, was even physically injured; and so on. All this can be observed in physical life if we do not run away from it, finding it unpleasant to observe the consequences of our deeds.

This, however, is only one side. Every action we do to human beings, or indeed to the other kingdoms of Nature, has another side. Let us assume that you do a good deed to another man. Such a deed has its existence and its significance in the spiritual world; it kindles warmth there; it is, in a sense, a source of spiritual rays of warmth. In the spiritual world 'soul-warmth' streams from a good deed, 'soul-coldness' from an evil deed done to other human beings. It is really as if one engendered warmth or coldness in the spiritual world according to one's behaviour to others. Other human actions act like bright, luminous rays in this or that direction in the spiritual world; others have a darkening effect. In short, one may say that we only really experience one half of what we accomplish in our life on earth.

Now, on attaining imaginative consciousness, what ordinary consciousness knows already, really vanishes. Whether a man is being helped or injured is for ordinary consciousness to recognise; but the effect of a deed, be it good or evil, wise or foolish, in the spiritual world—its warming or chilling, lightening or darkening action (there are manifold effects)—all this arises before imaginative consciousness and begins to be there for us. And we say to ourselves: Because you did not know all this when you let your ordinary consciousness function in your actions, it does not follow that it was not there. Do not imagine that what you did not know of in your actions—the sources of luminous and warming rays, etc.—was not there because you did not see or experience it. Do not imagine that. You have experienced it all in your sub-consciousness; you have been through it all. Just as the spiritual eyes of your higher consciousness see it now, so, while you were helping or harming another by your kind or evil deed, your sub-consciousness experienced its parallel significance for the spiritual world.

Further: when we have progressed and attained a sufficient intensification of imaginative consciousness we do not only gaze at the panorama of our experiences, but become perforce aware that we are not complete human beings until we have lived through this other aspect of our earthly actions, which had remained subconscious before. We begin to feel quite maimed in the face of this life-panorama that extends back to birth, or beyond it. It is as if something had been torn from us. We say to ourselves continually: You ought to have experienced that aspect too; you are really maimed, as if an eye or a leg had been removed. You have not really had one half of your experiences. This must arise in the course of imaginative consciousness; we must feel ourselves maimed in this way in respect to our experiences. Above all, we must feel that ordinary life is hiding something from us.

This feeling is especially intense in our present materialistic age. For men simply do not believe today that human actions have any value or significance beyond that for immediate life which takes its course in the physical world. It is regarded, more or less, as folly to declare that something else takes place in the spiritual world. Nevertheless, it is there. This feeling of being maimed comes before 'inspired' consciousness and one says to one's self: I must make it possible for myself to experience all I have failed to experience; yet this is almost impossible, except in a few details and to a very limited extent.

It is this tragic mood that weighs upon one who sees more

deeply into life. There is so much in life that we cannot fulfil on earth. In a sense, we must incur a debt to the future, admitting that life sets tasks which we cannot absolve in this present earthly life. We must owe them to the universe, saying: I shall only be able to experience that when I have passed through death. The Science of Initiation brings us this great, though often tragical enrichment of life; we feel this unavoidable indebtedness to life and recognise the necessity of owing the gods what we can only experience after death. Only then can we enter into an experience such as we owe to the universe.

This consciousness that our inner life must, in part, run its course by incurring debts to the future after death, leads to an immense deepening of human life. Spiritual science is not only there that we may learn this or that theoretically. He who studies it as one studies other things, would be better employed with a cookery book. Then, at least, he would be impelled to study in a more than theoretical manner, for life, chiefly the life of the stomach and all connected therewith, takes care that we take a cookery book more seriously than a mere theory. It is necessary for spiritual science, on approaching man, to deepen his life in respect to feeling.

Our life is immensely deepened when we become aware of our growing indebtedness to the gods and say: One half of our life on earth cannot really be lived, for it is hidden under the surface of existence. If, through initiation, we learn to know what is otherwise hidden from ordinary consciousness, we can see a little into the debts we have incurred. We then say: With ordinary consciousness we see we are incurring debts, but cannot read the 'promissory note' we ought to write. With initiation-consciousness we can, indeed, read the note, but cannot meet it in ordinary life. We must wait till death comes. And, when we have attained this consciousness, when we have so deepened our human conscience that this indebtedness is quite alive in us, we are ready to follow human life farther, beyond the retrospective tableau of which I have spoken and in which we reach back to birth. We now see that, after a few days, we must begin to experience what we have left un-experienced; and this holds for every single deed we have done to other human beings in the world. The last deeds

116

done before death are the first to come before us, and so backwards through life. We first become aware of what our last evil or good deeds signify for the world. Our experience of them while on earth is now eliminated; what we now experience is their significance for the world.

And then we go farther back, experiencing our life again, but backwards. We know that while doing this we are still connected with the earth, for it is only the other side of our deeds that we experience now.

We feel as if our life from now onwards were being borne in the womb of the universe. What we now experience is a kind of embryonic stage for our further life between death and a new birth; only, it is not borne by a mother but by the world, by all that we did not experience in physical life. We live through our physical life again, backwards and in its cosmic significance. We experience it now with a very divided consciousness. Living here in the physical world and observing the creatures around him, man feels himself pretty well as the lord of creation; and even though he calls the lion the king of beasts, he still feels himself, as a human being, superior. Man feels the creatures of the other kingdoms as inferior; he can judge them, but does not ascribe to them the power to judge him. He is above the other kingdoms of Nature.

He has a very different feeling, however, when after death he undergoes the experience I have just described. He no longer feels himself confronting the inferior kingdoms of Nature, but kingdoms of the spiritual world that are superior to him. He feels himself as the lowest kingdom, the others standing above him.

Thus, in undergoing all he has previously left unexperienced, man feels all around him beings far higher than himself. They unfold their sympathies and antipathies towards all he now lives through as a consequence of his earthly life. In this experience immediately after death we are within a kind of 'spiritual rain'. We live through the spiritual counterpart of our deeds, and the lofty beings who stand above us rain down their sympathies and antipathies. We are flooded by these, and feel in our spiritual being that what is illuminated by the sympathies of these lofty beings of the higher hierarchies will be accepted by the universe as a good element for the future; whereas all that encounters their antipathies will be rejected, for we feel it would be an evil element in the universe if we did not keep it to ourselves. The antipathies of these lofty beings rain down on an evil deed done to another human being, and we feel that the result would be something exceedingly bad for the universe if we released it, if we did not retain it in ourselves. So we gather up all that encounters the antipathies of these lofty beings. In this way we lay the foundation of our destiny, of all that works on into our next earthly life in order that it may find compensation through other deeds.

One can describe the passage of the human being through the soul-region after death from what I might call its more external aspect. I did this in my book *Theosophy*, where I followed more the accustomed lines of thought of our age. Now in this recapitulation within the General Anthroposophical Society I want to present a systematic statement of what Anthroposophy is, describing these things more inwardly. I want you to feel how man, in his inner being—in his human individuality—actually lives through the state after death.

Now when we understand these things in this way, we can again turn our attention to the world of dreams, and see it in a new light. Perceiving man's experience, after death, of the spiritual aspects of his earthly life, his deeds and thoughts, we can again turn to the dreaming man, to all he experiences when asleep. We now see that he has already lived through the above when asleep; but it remained quite unconscious. The difference between the experience in sleep and the experience after death becomes clear.

Consider man's life on earth. There are waking states interrupted again and again by sleep. Now a man who is not a 'sleepy-head' will spend about a third of his life asleep. During this third he does, in fact, live through the spiritual counterpart of his deeds; only, he knows nothing of it, his dreams merely casting up ripples to the surface. Much of the spiritual counterpart is perceived in dreams, but only in the form of weak surface-ripples. Nevertheless in deep sleep we do experience unconsciously the whole spiritual aspect of our daily life.

So we might put it this way: In our conscious daily life we experience what others think and feel, how they are helped or hindered by us; in sleep we experience unconsciously what the gods think about the deeds and thoughts of our waking life, though we know nothing of this. It is for this reason that one who sees into the secrets of life seems to himself so burdened with debt, so maimed—as I have described. All this has remained in the subconscious. Now after death it is really lived through consciously. For this reason man lives through the part of life he has slept through, i.e. about one-third, in time, of his earthly life. Thus, when he has passed through death, he lives through his nights again, backwards; only, what he lived through unconsciously, night by night, now becomes conscious.

We could even say—though it might almost seem as if we wanted to make fun of these exceedingly earnest matters: If one sleeps away the greater part of one's life, this retrospective experience after death will last longer; if one sleeps little, it will be shorter. On an average it will last a third of one's life, for one spends that in sleep. So if a man lives till the age of sixty, such experience after death will last twenty years. During this time he passes through a kind of embryonic stage for the spiritual world. Only after that will he be really free of the earth; then the earth no longer envelopes him, and he is born into the spiritual world. He escapes from the wrappings of earthly existence which he had borne around him until then, though in a spiritual sense, and feels this as his birth into the spiritual world.

Lecture 9

PHASES OF MEMORY AND THE REAL SELF

10th February, 1924

YOU have seen from the preceding lectures that a study of man's faculty of memory can give us valuable insight into the whole of human life and its cosmic connections. So today we will study this faculty of memory as such, in the various phases of its manifestation in human life, beginning with its manifestation in the ordinary consciousness that man has between birth and death.

What man experiences in concrete, everyday life, in thinking, feeling and willing, in unfolding his physical forces, too—all this he transforms into memories which he recalls from time to time.

But if you compare the shadowy character of these memory-pictures, whether spontaneous or deliberately sought, with the robust experiences to which they refer, you will say that they exist as mere thoughts or mental presentations; you are led to call memories just 'pictures'. Nevertheless, it is these pictures that we retain in our ego from our experiences in the outer world; in a sense, we bear them with us as the treasure won from experience. If a part of these memories should be lost—as in certain pathological cases of which I have already spoken—our ego itself suffers injury. We feel that our innermost being, our ego, has been damaged if it must forfeit this or that from its treasury of memories, for it is this treasury that makes our life a complete whole. One could also point to the very serious conditions that sometimes result in cases of apoplectic stroke when certain portions of the patient's past life are obliterated from his memory.

Moreover, when we survey from a given moment our life since our last birth, we must feel our memories as a connected whole if we are to regard ourselves rightly as human souls. These few features indicate the role of the faculty of memory in physical, earthly life. But its role is far greater still. What would the external world with all its impressions constantly renewed, with all it gives us, however vividly—what would it be to us if we could not link new impressions to the memories of past ones! Last, but not least, we may say that, after all, all learning consists in linking new impressions to the content borne in memory. A great part of educational method depends on finding the most rational way of linking the new things we have to teach the children to what we can draw from their store of memories.

In short, whenever we have to bring the external world to the soul, to evoke the soul's own life that it may feel and experience inwardly its own existence, we appeal to memory in the last resort. So we must say that, on earth, memory constitutes the most important and most comprehensive part of man's inner life.

Let us now study memory from yet another point of view. It is quite easy to see that the sum of memories we bear within us is really a fragment. We have forgotten so much in the course of life; but there are moments, frequently abnormal, when what has been long forgotten comes before us again. These are especially such moments in which a man comes near to death and many things emerge that have long been far from his conscious memory. Old people, when dying, suddenly remember things that had long disappeared from their conscious memory. Moreover, if we study dreams really intimately—and they, too, link on to memory— we find things arising which have quite certainly been experienced, but they passed us by unnoticed. Nevertheless, they are in our soul life, and arise in sleep when the hindrances of the physical and etheric organism are not acting and the astral body and ego are alone. We do not usually notice these things and so fail to observe that conscious memory is but a fragment of all we receive; in the course of life we take in much in the same form, only, it is received into the subconscious directly, where it is inwardly elaborated.

Now, as long as we are living on earth, we continue to regard the memories that arise from the depths of our soul in the form of thoughts as the essential part of memory. Thoughts of past experience come and go. We search for them. We regard that as the essence of memory.

However, when we go through the gate of death our life on earth is followed by a few days in which pictures of the life just ended come before us in a gigantic perspective. These pictures are suddenly there: the events of years long past and of the last few days are there simultaneously. As the spatial exists side by side and only possesses spatial perspective, so the temporal events of our earthly life are now seen side by side and possess 'time-perspective'. This tableau appears suddenly, but, during the short time it is there, it becomes more and more shadowy, weaker and weaker. Whereas in earthly life we look into ourselves and feel that we have our memory-pictures 'rolled up' within us, *these* pictures now become greater and greater. We feel as if they were being received by the universe. What is at first comprised within the memory tableau as in a narrow space, becomes greater and greater, more and more shadowy, until we find it has expanded to a universe, becoming so faint that we can scarcely decipher what we first saw plainly. We can still divine it; then it vanishes in the far spaces and is no longer there.

That is the second form taken by memory—in a sense, its second metamorphosis—in the first few days after death. It is the phase which we can describe as the flight of our memories out into the cosmos. And all that, like memory, we have bound so closely to our life between birth and death, expands and becomes more and more shadowy, to be finally lost in the wide spaces of the cosmos.

It is really as if we saw what we have actually been calling our ego during earthly life, disappear into the wide spaces of the cosmos. This experience lasts a few days and, when these have passed, we feel that we ourselves are being expanded too. Between birth and death we feel ourselves within our memories; and now we actually feel ourselves within these rapidly retreating memories and being received into the wide spaces of the universe.

After we have suffered this supersensible stupor, **or** faintness, which takes from us the sum-total of our memories and our inner consciousness of earthly life, we live in the third phase of memory. This third phase of memory teaches us that what we had called ourself during earthly life—in virtue of our memories —has spread itself through the wide spaces of the universe, thereby proving its insubstantiality for us. If we were only what can be preserved in our memories between birth and death, we would be nothing at all a few days after death.

But we now enter a totally different element. We have realised that we cannot retain our memories, for the world takes them from us after death. But there is something objective behind all the memories we have harboured during earthly life. The spiritual counterpart, of which I spoke yesterday, is engraved into the world; and it is this counterpart of our memories that we now enter. Between birth and death we have experienced this or that with this or that person or plant or mountain spring, with all we have approached during life. There is no single experience whose spiritual counterpart is not engraved into the spiritual world in which we are ever present, even while on earth. Every hand-shake we have exchanged has its spiritual counterpart; it is there, inscribed into the spiritual world. Only while we are surveying our life in the first days after death do we have these pictures of our life before us. These conceal, to a certain extent, what we have inscribed into the world through our deeds, thoughts and feelings.

The moment we pass through the gate of death to this other 'life', we are at once filled with the content of our life-tableau, i.e. with pictures which extend, in perspective, back to birth and even beyond. But all this vanishes into the wide cosmic spaces and we now see the spiritual counter-images of all the deeds we have done since birth. All the spiritual counter-images we have experienced (unconsciously, in sleep) become visible, and in such a way that we are immediately impelled to retrace our steps and go through all these experiences once more. In ordinary life, when we go from Dornach to Basle we know we can go from Basle to Dornach, for we have in the physical world an appropriate conception of space. But in ordinary consciousness we do not know, when we go from birth to death, that we can also go from death to birth. As in the physical world one can go from Dornach to Basle and return from Basle to Dornach, so we go from birth to death during earthly life, and, after death, can return from death to birth.

This is what we do in the spiritual world when we experience backwards the spiritual counter-images of all we have undergone during earthly life. Suppose you have had an experience with something in the external realm of Nature—let us say, with a tree. You have observed the tree or, as a woodman, cut it down. Now all this has its spiritual counterpart; above all, whether you have merely observed the tree, or cut it down, or done something else to it, has its significance for the whole universe. What you can experience with the physical tree you experience in physical, earthly life; *now*, as you go backwards from death to birth, it is the spiritual counterpart of this experience that you live through.

If, however, our experience was with another human being—if, for example, we have caused him pain—there is already a spiritual counterpart in the physical world; only, it is not our experience: it is the pain experienced by the other man. Perhaps the fact that we were the cause of his pain gave us a certain feeling of satisfaction; we may have been moved by a feeling of revenge or the like. Now, on going backwards through our life, we do not undergo *our* experience, but *his*. We experience what he experienced through our deed. That, too, is a part of the spiritual counterpart and is inscribed into the spiritual world. In short, man lives through his experiences once more, but in a spiritual way, going backwards from death to birth.

As I said yesterday, it is a part of this experience to feel that beings whom, for the present, we may call 'superhuman', are participating in it. Pressing onwards through these spiritual counterparts of our experiences, we feel as if these spiritual beings were showering down their sympathies and antipathies upon our deeds and thoughts, as we experience them backwards. Thereby we feel what each deed done by us on earth, each thought, feeling, or impulse of will, is worth for purely spiritual existence. In bitter pain we experience the harmfulness of some deed we have done. In burning thirst we experience the passions we have harboured in our soul; and this continues until we have sufficiently realised the worthlessness, for the spiritual world, of harbouring passions and have outgrown these states which depend on our physical, earthly personality.

At this point of our studies we can see where the boundary

between the psychical and the physical really is. You see, we can easily regard things like thirst or hunger as physical. But I ask you to imagine that the same physical changes that are in your organism when you are thirsty were in a body not ensouled. The same changes could be there, but the soulless body would not suffer thirst. As a chemist you might investigate the changes in your body when you are thirsty. But if, by some means, you could produce these same changes, in the same substances and in the same complex of forces, in a body without a soul, it would not suffer thirst. Thirst is not something in the body; it lives in the soul—in the astral—through changes in the physical body. It is the same with hunger. And if someone, in his soul, takes great pleasure in something that can only be satisfied by physical measures in physical life, it is as if he were experiencing thirst in physical life; the psychical part of him feels thirst, burning thirst, for those things which he was accustomed to satisfy by physical means. For one cannot carry out physical functions when the physical body has been laid aside. Man must first accustom himself to live in his psycho-spiritual being without his physical body; and a great part of the backward journey I have described is concerned with this. At first he experiences continually burning thirst for what can only be gratified through a physical body. Just as the child must accustom himself to use his organs—must learn to speak, for example—so man between death and a new birth must accustom himself to do without his physical body as the foundation of his psychical experiences. He must grow into the spiritual world.

There are descriptions of this experience which, as I said yesterday, lasts one-third of the time of physical life, which depict it as a veritable hell. For example, if you read descriptions like those given in the literature of the Theosophical Society where, following oriental custom, this life is called Kamaloka, they will certainly make your flesh creep. Well, these experiences are not like that. They can appear so if you compare them directly with earthly life, for they are something to which we are so utterly unaccustomed. We must suddenly adapt ourselves to the spiritual counter-images and counter-values of our earthly experience. What we felt on earth as pleasure, is there privation, bitter privation, and, strictly speaking, only our unsatisfying, painful or sorrowful experiences on earth are satisfying there. In many respects that is somewhat horrible when compared with earthly life; but we simply cannot compare it with earthly life directly, for it is not experienced here but in the life after death where we do not judge with earthly conceptions.

So when, for example, you experience after death the pain of another man through having caused him pain on earth, you say to yourself at once: 'If I did not feel this pain, I would remain an imperfect human soul, for the pain I have caused in the universe would continually take something from me. I only become a whole human being by experiencing this compensation."

It may cost us a struggle to see that pain experienced after death in return for pain caused to another, is really a blessing. It will depend on the inner constitution of our soul whether we find this difficult or not; but there is a certain state of soul in which this painful compensation for many things done on earth is even experienced as bliss. It is the state of soul that results from acquiring on earth some knowledge of the supersensible life. We feel that, through this painful compensation, we are perfecting our human being, while, without it, we should fall short of full human stature. If you have caused another pain, you are of less value than before; so, if you judge reasonably, you will say: In face of the universe I am a worse human soul after causing pain to another than before. You will feel it a blessing that you are able, after death, to compensate for this pain by experiencing it yourself.

That, my dear friends, is the third phase of memory. At first what we have within us as memory is condensed to pictures, which last some days after death; then it is scattered through the universe, your whole inner life in the form of thoughts returning thereto. But while we lose the memories locked up within us during earthly life—while these seek the cosmic spaces—the world, from out of all we have spiritually engraved upon it, gives us back to ourselves in objective form.

There is scarcely a stronger proof of man's intimate connection with the world than this; that after death, in regard to our inner life, we have first to lose ourselves, in order to be given back to ourselves from out of the universe. And we experience this, even in the face of painful events, as something that belongs to our human being as a whole. We do, indeed, feel that the world takes to itself the inner life we possessed here, and gives back to us again what we have engraved upon it. It is just the part we did not notice, the part we passed by but inscribed upon spiritual existence with clear strokes, that gives us our own self again. Then, as we retrace our life backwards through birth and beyond, we reach out into the wide spaces of spiritual existence.

It is only now, after having undergone all this, that we enter the spiritual world and are really able to live there. Our faculty of memory now undergoes its fourth metamorphosis. We feel that everywhere behind the ordinary memory of earthly life something has been living in us, though we were not aware of it. It has engraved itself into the world and now we, ourselves, become it. We have received our earthly life in its spiritual significance; we now become this significance. After travelling back through birth to the spiritual world we find ourselves confronting it in a very peculiar way. In a sense, we ourselves in our spiritual counterpart—in our true spiritual worth—now confront the world. We have passed through the above experiences, have experienced the pain caused to another, have experienced the spiritual value corresponding to an experience with a tree, let us say; we have experienced all this, but it was not self-experience. We might compare this with the embryonic stage of human life; for then—and even throughout the first years of life—all we experience does not yet reach the level of self-consciousness, which only awakens gradually.

Thus, when we enter the spiritual world, all we have experienced backwards gradually becomes ourself, our spiritual self-consciousness. We are now what we have experienced; we are our own spiritual worth corresponding thereto. With this existence, that really represents the other side of our earthly existence, we enter the world that contains nothing of the ordinary kingdoms of external Nature—mineral, plant and animal kingdoms—for these belong to the earth. But in that world there immediately come before us, first, the souls of those who have died before us and to whom we stood in some kind of relationship, and then the individualities of higher spiritual beings.

We live as spirit among human and non-human spirits, and this environment of spiritual individualities is now our world. The relationship of these spiritual individualities, human or non-human, to ourselves now constitutes our experience. As on earth we have our experience with the beings of the external kingdoms of Nature, so now, with spiritual beings of different ranks. And it is especially important that we have felt their sympathies and antipathies like spiritual rain—to use yesterday's metaphor—permeating these experiences during the retrospective part of the life between death and birth that I have described to you schematically. We now stand face to face with these beings of whom we previously perceived only their sympathies and antipathies while we were living through the spiritual counterpart of our earthly life: we live among these beings now that we have reached the spiritual world. We gradually feel as if inwardly permeated with force, with impulses proceeding from the spiritual beings around us. All that we have previously experienced now becomes more and more real to us, in a spiritual way. We gradually feel as if standing in the light or shadow of these beings in whom we are beginning to live. Before, through living through the spiritual worth corresponding to some earthly experience, we felt this or that about it, found it valuable or harmful to the cosmos. We now feel: There is something I have done on earth, in thought or deed; it has its corresponding spiritual worth, and this is engraved into the spiritual cosmos. The beings whom I now encounter can either do something with it, or not; it either lies in the direction of their evolution or of the evolution for which they are striving, or it does not. We feel ourselves placed before the beings of the spiritual world and realise that we have acted in accordance with their intentions or against them, have either added to, or subtracted from, what they willed for the evolution of the world.

Above all, it is no mere ideal judgment of ourselves that we feel, but a real evaluation; and this evaluation is itself the reality of our existence when we enter the spiritual world after death.

When you have done something wrong as a man in the physical world, you condemn it yourself if you have sufficient conscience and reason; or it is condemned by the law, or by the judge, or by other men who despise you for it. But you do not grow thin on this account—at least, not very thin, unless you are quite specially constituted. On entering the world of spiritual beings, however, we do not merely meet the ideal judgment that we are of little worth in respect of any fault or disgraceful deed we have committed; we feel the gaze of these beings resting upon us as if it would annihilate our very being. In respect of all we have done that is valuable, the gaze of these beings falls upon us as if we first attained thereby our full reality as psycho-spiritual beings. Our reality depends upon our value. Should we have hindered the evolution that was intended in the spiritual world, it is as if darkness were robbing us of our very existence. If we have done something in accordance with the evolution of the spiritual world, and its effects continue, it is as if light were calling us to fresh spiritual life. We experience all I have described and enter the realm of spiritual beings. This enhances our consciousness in the spiritual world and keeps us awake. Through all the demands made upon us there, we realise that we have won something in the universe in regard to our own reality.

Suppose we have done something that hinders the evolution of the world and can only arouse the antipathy of the spiritual beings whose realm we now enter. The after-effect takes its course as I have described and we feel our consciousness darken; stupefaction ensues, sometimes complete extinction of consciousness. We must now wake up again. On doing so, we feel in regard to our spiritual existence as if someone were cutting into our flesh in the physical world; only, this experience in the spiritual is much more real—though it is real enough in the physical world. In short, what we are in the spiritual world proves to be the result of what we ourselves have initiated. You see from this that man has sufficient inducement to return again to earthly life.

Why to return? Well, through what he has engraved into the spiritual world man has himself experienced all he has done for good or ill in earthly life; and it is only by returning to earth that he can actually compensate for what, after all, he has only learnt to know through earthly experience. In fact, when he reads his value for the world in the countenances of these spiritual beings— to put it metaphorically—he is sufficiently impelled to return, when able, to the physical world, in order to live his life in a different way from before. Many incapacities for this he will still retain, and only after many lives on earth will full compensation really be possible.

If we look into ourselves during earthly life, we find, at first, memories. It is of these that, to begin with, we build our soul-life when we shut out the external world; and it is upon these alone that the creative imagination of the artist draws. That is the first form of memory. Behind it are the mighty 'pictures' which become perceptible immediately after we have passed through the gate of death. These are taken from us: they expand to the wide spaces of the universe. When we survey our memory-pictures we can say that there lives behind them something that at once proceeds towards the cosmic spaces when our body is taken from us. Through our body we hold together what is really seeking to become 'ideal' in the universe. But while we go through life and retain memories of our experiences, we leave behind in the world something still further behind our memories. We leave it behind us in the course of time and must experience it again as we retrace our steps. This lies behind our memory as a third 'structure'. First, we have the tapestry of memory; behind it, the mighty cosmic pictures we have 'rolled up' within us; behind this, again, lives what we have written into the world. Not until we have lived through this are we really ourselves, standing naked in spirit before the spiritual universe which clothes us in its garments when we enter it.

We must, indeed, look at our memories if we want to get gradually beyond the transient life of man. Our earthly memories are transient and become dispersed through the universe. But our Self lives behind them: the Self that is given us again from out of the spiritual world that we may find our way from time to eternity.

Further Information

RUDOLF STEINER (1861–1925) was the founder of anthroposophy, a modern spiritual path or science. From his spiritual researches he was able to provide indications for the renewal of many human activities, including education (Waldorf Schools), agriculture (Biodynamics), medicine (Anthroposophical Medicine), special education (the Camphill Movement), economics, philosophy, the arts and religion. He wrote some 30 books and delivered over 6000 lectures to audiences all over Europe and Scandinavia, and in 1924 founded the General Anthroposophical Society, which today has branches throughout the world.

Basic books and related works

How to Know Higher Worlds
A new translation of the classic account of the Western esoteric path of initiation. It began appearing in instalments in 1904, the first time this information was made public, adapted and transformed for the consciousness of our times. It was presented for all those who sought to know the realities of the spiritual world while fulfilling and even perfecting their daily duties in practical life. His advice is practical, clear and powerful. Trans: C. Bamford. 288 pp. GA10.

0 88010 372 8 paperback

Knowledge of the Higher Worlds: How is it Achieved?
An earlier translation of *How to Know Higher Worlds*, in a smaller, pocket-sized format. More than 50,000 sold in English. Trans: G. Metaxa, rev: D.S. Osmond, C. Davy. 224 pp. GA10.

1 85584 002 2 hardback
0 85440 221 7 paperback

Occult Science: An Outline
One of the 20th century's most profound works on the relation of man to the spiritual worlds and his history on earth. With the rigorous method of a scientist, Steiner describes the nature of man, life between death and rebirth, and includes a panoramic view of the spiritually guided evolution of man from the earlier planetary phases to the present day, the fifth Post-Atlantean epoch, and into the future. Includes a detailed chapter on exercises of spiritual self development and initiation. Trans: G. and M. Adams. 352 pp. GA13.

0 85440 207 1 hardback
0 85440 440 6 paperback

Theosophy — An Introduction to the Spiritual Processes in Human Life and in the Cosmos
This is a new translation of the work in which Rudolf Steiner turns his philosophically trained scientific mind to the precise description of his own supersensible experiences and the supersensible phenomena revealed by them. It is a key work for anyone seeking a solid grounding in spiritual reality. Trans: C.E. Creeger. 256 pp. GA9.

0 88010 373 6 paperback

Thinking as a Spiritual Path: A Philosophy of Freedom
A new translation of Steiner's central philosophical work, and the one that he himself believed would have the longest life and the greatest spiritual and cultural consequences. Written just one hundred years ago as a phenomenological account of 'results of observing the human soul according to the methods of natural science,' this seminal work asserts that free spiritual activity — understood as the human ability to think and act independently of physical nature — is the appropriate and available path for human beings today to gain true knowledge of themselves and of the universe. Trans: M. Lipson. 228 pp. GA4.

0 88010 385 X paperback

The Philosophy of Spiritual Activity: A Philosophy of Freedom
Are we free or determined by external conditions? What is freedom? This book presents Steiner's profound exploration of these ultimate questions of human existence. Starting with a discussion of what knowledge is and what makes it possible, Steiner leads us to an understanding of the experience of thinking, a uniquely human experience of ourselves as spiritual beings, and ends by indicating how true morality can become the basis for our actions. This book can lead the reader to the experience of living thinking – new thinking – by which all human activity may be renewed. Trans: R. Stebbing. 195 pp. GA4.

1 85584 000 6 hardback
1 85584 001 4 paperback

Christianity as Mystical Fact
In this work Steiner drew attention to how the Mysteries of antiquity, those of the pagan wisdom, the Greek sages and the ancient Egyptians, led to their culmination in the incarnation of Christ and the Mystery of Golgotha. Christianity, however, was not a further development of what had existed in the Mysteries, but something new and unique, and Steiner describes the profundity of the Christ event, the turning point in human evolution, in chapters on the Gospels, the Lazarus miracle and the Apocalypse of John. He relates how 'Christianity brought the content of the Mysteries out of the obscurity of the temple into the clear light of day'. Trans: C. Davy, A. Bittleston. 155 pp. GA8.

0 85440 256 X paperback

A Road to Self-knowledge and the Threshold of the Spiritual World
These 24 essays amplify that described in *Knowledge of the Higher Worlds*,
and form meditations for the reader to work on, 'leading to a real inner work
of the soul...bringing about in the soul...that about which they speak'.
Subjects include the physical, etheric and astral bodies, the ego, repeated
earth lives, spiritual beings, thinking and meditation. Trans: H. Collison, rev:
M. Cotterell. 174 pp. GA16/17.

0 85440 291 8 paperback

Truth-Wrought Words
Verses by Rudolf Steiner from *Wahrspruchworte*, with the original German on
facing pages, verses for children, verses for the dead, two renderings of the
Foundation Stone Mantra, verse passages from the Mystery Plays, a translation
of the *Dream Song of Olaf Åsteson* and a section of quotations concerning Beauty,
Truth and Goodness. An excellent selection of thought-provoking ideas and
imaginations, rich in content and ideal for repeated study. Trans: A. MacKaye
Ege. 209 pp.

0 910142 82 3 hardback

Books on anthroposophy and nearly all of Rudolf Steiner's works in English
translation are available through the publishers of this book. Please write to:

Rudolf Steiner Press, PO Box 955, Bristol BS99 5QN, Great Britain

or

Anthroposophic Press
RR4, Box 94-A1, Hudson, NY 122534, United States of America

Distributors in other English-language countries are:

Australia   Rudolf Steiner Book Centre,
                   307 Sussex Street, Sydney, NSW 2000

Canada   Tri-fold Books,
                   81 Lawton Blvd., Toronto, Ontario M4V 1Z6

New Zealand   Steinerbooks (NZ)
                   181 Ladies Mile, Box 11-336, Ellerslie, Auckland 5

South Africa   Rudolf Steiner Publications SA
                   PO Box 4891, Randburg 2125

Books both in and out of print are available from the Library of the
Anthroposophical Society in Great Britain. Please write to:

Anthroposophical Society in Great Britain
35 Park Road, London NW1 6XT, Great Britain

Information on, and contact addresses for, practical activities in Great
Britain are also available from the Society.